FIFE
FOLK TALES

D1388396

SHEILA KINNINMONTH

ILLUSTRATED BY JONATHAN DOWLING

The
History
Press

First published 2017

The History Press
The Mill, Brimscombe Port
Stroud, Gloucestershire, GL5 2QG
www.thehistorypress.co.uk

Text © Sheila Kinninmonth, 2017
Illustrations © Jonathan Dowling, 2017

The right of Sheila Kinninmonth to be identified as the Author
of this work has been asserted in accordance with the
Copyright, Designs and Patents Act 1988.

British Library Cataloguing in Publication Data.
A catalogue record for this book is available from the British Library.

ISBN 978 0 7509 6753 2

Typesetting and origination by The History Press
Printed in Great Britain

CONTENTS

FOREWORD

The folk tales of Fife are a treasure chest lovingly guarded by families throughout the Kingdom and told round the fireside in Scots. This collection is from families, farmworkers, fisher-folk, weavers, millers, miners and blacksmiths. Such were my family and Sheila's.

Family get-togethers, funerals, weddings and especially the 'Big Holiday', New Year, were the times for sharing. In the days before mass media, families celebrated their own accomplishments. Food, drink, music and stories were all shared. This warmth pervaded the cold and dark of the winter months. Everyone had a part to play, whether it was a song ('Sing that one I like Mary, it always brings a tear to my eye'), a poem ('Give us one of your verses, Archie'), a tune on the fiddle, pipes, or melodeon, or one of the more portable instruments, jaws harp, mouthorgan or spoons, or a story ('Tell us about the time you fell asleep in the graveyard, Andy').

Patterns were set up which lasted for the rest of life. We listened and picked up the story shape and delivery and we knew the stories we would like to tell. Now in her nineties, Sheila's mother can still remember the stories and the songs.

This collection is the Folk of Fife's book so wire in to the feast which has been laid out for you.

Senga Munro MBE
Storyteller and Tradition Bearer

ACKNOWLEDGEMENTS

First I'd like to thank the talented Jonathan Dowling (jonathan-dowlingart.co.uk) for agreeing to tackle the illustrations for the book. I know a lot of what I asked for was out of his comfort zone but he rose to the challenge well.

Then there's my mum, Cath Ferrier (*née* Mitchell), and those of the Mitchell clan who shared the stories and planted the story seeds all those years ago. Also thanks to my mother-in-law, Liza Kinninmonth, who shared her tales of Kemback.

Also I'd like to thank all the kind folk I've met in the last year through the Fife Family History Society and Fife Writes who were willing to talk to me and give me snippets of remembered tales. I'd especially like to thank the lady who was in the opposite bed from me in hospital last year. I had my laptop with me and was working away when she asked what I was doing. When I told her she shared the story of Green Jean. She and her family had owned the house at one time and still lived nearby so she knew the story well, but no, she hadn't actually seen the ghost.

I'd also like to thank the extremely helpful librarians in Cupar, Dunfermline, Kirkcaldy and Buckhaven libraries who helped me track down several old books and manuscripts that hadn't seen the light of day for years and who opened their special cupboards and let me browse.

Then there are the authors of these old books themselves who took the trouble in centuries gone by to listen to and write down the stories they heard. People like the Revd Peter Chalmers, Ebenezer Henderson, John Jack, the Revd Andrew Small, the Revd Walter Wood and James Wilkie.

And last but not least I'd like to thank my fellow storytellers, especially Senga Munro, Sylvia Troon, Robbie Fotheringham, Kate Walker and the rest of the Blether Tay-gither and Burgh Blethers gang for their unstinting support and encouragement. Also storyteller Linda Williamson who gave me permission to retell a couple of stories I had heard her late husband, traveller Duncan Williamson, tell many years ago when he lived in Fife.

INTRODUCTION

Fife may be Scotland's smallest region but the 'Kingdom', as it is still proudly known, lies at the heart of Scotland, the right to be known as a Kingdom fiercely defended because of its long association with the Scottish monarchy. From earliest times it had been the centre of power and is of historical significance, having witnessed many of the pivotal events of Scotland's history. Fife is home to Dunfermline, once Scotland's capital, and St Andrews, an early seat of learning and, at one time, the focal point of the religious life of the nation, housing the bones of the nation's patron saint.

Man came early to settle in Fife. About 8,000 years ago, when the entire population of Scotland numbered only a few hundred, a strip of coastline in North Fife was one of the rare abodes of those Stone-Age settlers, the Mesolithic folk. Later, in Neolithic times and through the long centuries of the Bronze Age, the population was steadily growing. And then, almost 2,400 years ago, a great wave of invaders from the Continent, the Gaelic-speaking Celts, swept triumphantly into Scotland to start a new Iron Age of progress. Their first foothold was on the shores of the River Tay. And up the estuary, where the hills of North Fife and Perthshire meet, the invaders covered the summits with forts that are still clearly visible.

Centuries later the early Christian missionaries arrived. One, a monk called St Rule from Patras in western Greece, brought a human arm bone, three fingers from a right hand, one tooth and a kneecap, all genuine parts of the skeleton of St Andrew. People liked a piece of a saint in those days. He is said to have established a church there which was to become the new resting place for the relics. Folk didn't know much about him, this stranger from a faraway land, but all that mattered was the powerful symbol his bones represented.

Throughout the Middle Ages the Earls of Fife were first among the nobility of Scotland. They had hereditary right to place the crown on the King's head at his coronation and to lead his army into battle.

St Andrews in Fife was an important religious centre, the cathedral being by far the largest in Scotland and also being the home of the Archbishop of St Andrews, Scotland's leading churchman.

Fife was also a seat of learning. St Andrews University was founded in 1411, after which higher education thrived for the first time in Scotland at Falkland Palace, a favourite amongst the Scottish Kings for centuries.

Fife is a peninsula surrounded by the North Sea to the east, the Firth of Forth to the south and the Firth of Tay to the north. James VI was said to have described it as 'A beggar's mantle fringed with gold', alluding to the rich trading possibilities afforded by the coastline as opposed to what was at the time boggy, unimproved and unremarkable though pleasant farmland away from the coast.

Fife in those days was noted not just for its palaces, its churchmen and its scholars. It was equally famed for its rich merchants and its thriving trade with the European Continent. All along the East Neuk coast, crowded hard against each other were the Royal Burghs that specialized in this overseas trade. In addition to the merchants and seamen on their peaceful missions, Fife produced a special breed of sea dogs who fought the pirates of England for their Scottish shipmasters.

Those East Neuk ports were prosperous, with sturdy little houses beside the sea-wall or up narrow wynds that led so often from the shore to the High Street far above it. It was the fisher-folk who lived in the wynds, the sea captains and the merchants had more spacious mansions, while the lairds loved the safety of castles.

It was also in Fife that Alexander III plunged to his death; Macduff fled from Macbeth; Robert the Bruce's parents courted; King Malcolm met his beloved Margaret; Mary of Lorraine landed at Balcomie; Sir Henry Wood trounced Henry VIII's navy between Crail and the May Island; Andrew Selkirk, alias Robinson Crusoe, sailed from Largo; the Spanish survivors of the Armada put into Anstruther; Cardinal Beaton was slung into an unknown grave near Kilrenny; and James V crossed the wee Dreel Burn in Anstruther on the back of a Fife fishwife.

From Pictish relics, to cathedrals and royal palaces, pictur-esque villages and great castles, history is but a step away in the Kingdom of Fife. For many a century no other place in Scotland was quite as exciting to live in and it still has a herit-age that is unique, though over 400 years have passed since the height of its fame.

And this history and heritage, along with Fife's varied landscape, is where the folk tales come from. Here are tales of haunted castles, mansions, caves and hillsides. Tales of Kings and lairds, magic and superstition, shipwrecks and smugglers, saints, sinners and rogues, strange folk and wise fools all told round the fire of cottar, house and mansion alike. Here too are tales which probably travelled across the sea with the invaders and traders and became embedded in Fife culture.

I was born, grew up and still live in North East Fife and remember hearing many of the stories from this part of the region when I was a child. My mother and grandparents, as their parents and grandparents before them, liked to share stories and music round the fire of an evening and at family gatherings. My grandfather was one of a family of nine so my mother had lots of cousins, many of whom seemed to play instruments, sing songs, write and recite poetry and tell stories. These weren't well read, literate folk but ordinary farm workers carrying on the oral traditions. With this background it's no wonder I became a storyteller myself. It was while working in Early Years education that I discovered first Senga Munro, a fine traditional storyteller, and then about ten years ago, the Scottish Storytelling Centre in Edinburgh. It was through them I was able to hone my natural storytelling skills and expand my repertoire. With Senga's encouragement and that of fellow members of the Blether Tay-gither storytelling group in Dundee I was able to apply and be accepted onto the Centre's Directory of Storytellers.

I have tried to write the stories as I would tell them, using my natural tongue from time to time, though as other storytellers will know, each retelling is different from the last. Please take the stories, make them your own and tell them, they're not meant to stay static on the page but should be shared.

Sheila Kinninmonth, 2017

1

GIANTS, FAIRIES AND BROONIES

THE HISTORY OF KITTY ILL-PRETTS

There once was a poor woman living in Fife who had three daughters, the youngest of whom was called Kitty. On her deathbed the woman called her daughters to her to say goodbye. She didn't have much to leave them except an auld pat, an auld pan, half a bannock and her blessing. She gave the auld pat to her eldest, the auld pan to the second while all she gave Kitty was the bannock and her blessing. She also told them to go to the King's house to look for work.

So the daughters set off for the King's house but the older girls were so jealous of Kitty they tried to chase her home. However, Kitty wasn't to be chased off and she went to the palace too. When they got there the King himself came out to greet them so they asked him for work.

'What can you do?' he asked.

'I can shew mony a braw thing,' said the eldest.

'I can bake mony a braw thing,' said the second.

'I can do all that they can do and much more besides,' said Kitty.

So they were given work but after a while the King noticed that Kitty was far cleverer than her sisters. So one day he came to her and said, 'Kitty, I'd like you to help me get something I really want. There is a giant near here over the Bridge of a Hair who owns a wonderful sword called the Sword of Light which can light your way in the dark without a lantern. I would be happy if I had that sword and if you were to get it for me I'd marry my eldest son to your eldest sister.'

Now this was a dangerous and difficult task but Kitty was determined to try. So she filled her apron with salt and set off over the Bridge of a Hair to the giant's house. She found him there, stirring a great pot of porridge on the kitchen fire and as he stirred he kept stopping and tasting it to see if it was right. When Kitty saw this she climbed on the roof and threw a handful of salt down the kitchen chimney into the porridge pot. Next time the giant tasted it he said, 'Its ower saut, its ower saut,' but he kept on stirring and tasting and Kitty kept throwing down the salt until the giant called for a servant to fetch some water from the well to put in the pot. As it was

dark he told him to take the Sword of Light. So the servant took a pitcher and the sword and set off to the well. Kitty followed him and when he bent over the well she pushed him in, snatched the sword and ran off as fast as she could. The giant wondered why the servant was taking so long so he looked out and saw Kitty running away with his sword. He tried to chase after her but he knew his weight would break the Bridge of a Hair down. So the King got his sword and her eldest sister married the prince as promised.

The King was happy for a while but one day he asked Kitty if she could help him again. 'That same giant,' he said, 'has a most beautiful horse in his stable with a saddle all decorated with silver bells. I would be so happy if I had that horse and saddle, that I would marry my second son to your second sister.'

'Well,' said Kitty, 'I'll try.' This time she filled her apron with straw and set off for the Bridge of a Hair again. When she got to the giant's house she found the beautiful horse and saddle. She went round the horse stuffing straw into every bell so they wouldn't tinkle. When she thought all the bells were stuffed she got up on the horse and rode away as fast as she could. Unfortunately she had missed a bell so it tinkled when she moved. The giant heard and tried to catch her but he knew the bridge wouldn't take his weight. So the King got his beautiful horse and saddle and the second sister married a prince too.

The King was happy for a long time but eventually he came to Kitty again and said, 'I can't be really happy till I get one more thing. The giant has a beautiful bedcover all decorated with precious stones. If I had that I would marry you myself.'

So Kitty said she would do what she could and again set off for the giant's house. This time she went in and hid under his bed. The giant and his wife soon went to bed and fell asleep. Then Kitty stretched out her hand from under the bed and gave the cover a great pull but it was heavy and wouldn't move.

The giant woke up and soon found Kitty under the bed and dragged her out saying, 'Now Kitty, if you were me and I was you what would you do to me?' You see he was a bit stupid, though he was big, and had to ask Kitty how he should punish her.

'Well,' said Kitty, 'I would make a great big bowl of porridge and make you eat it till it was coming out your eyes and ears and nose. Then I would put you in a sack and tie it up, then go out and cut down a tree and bring it home and beat the sack till you were dead.'

'Well,' said the giant, 'that's just what I'll do.' He made the porridge and gave Kitty a spoon to eat it with but when he wasn't looking she poured it over her head so it looked like it was coming out of her eyes and ears and nose. Then the stupid giant put her in a sack and tied it up with string and went out to the forest to cut down a tree to beat her with. But Kitty had a knife so when the giant went out she cut a hole in the sack and crept out. Then she sewed up the hole, caught the giant's wife, his servants, his cow, his pig, his cat and his dog and put them in the sack and tied it up again. Then she grabbed the bedcover and ran off over the Bridge of a Hair back to the palace.

By and by the giant came home and began beating the sack. Well there was such a noise. His wife screamed, the servants roared, the cow lowed, the pigs squealed, the dog barked and the cat mewed, all crying out, 'It's me, it's me!' The stupid giant just said, 'I ken it's you!' and carried on beating. Eventually all went quiet and he opened the sack. What a rage he was in when he saw what he'd done. He put on his boots and ran after Kitty as fast as he could but she had a good start and was safely on the other side of the bridge sitting on the bank.

'Kitty, tell me how I can get over to you?' yelled the daft giant and Kitty answered, 'Go and get a rope and tie a boulder on to the end of it and your purse to the middle of it then throw it to me and I'll pull you over the river.'

So the giant did as Kitty said and threw the end with the boulder on it over to Kitty and held on to the other end himself. Well Kitty pulled and pulled the rope till she got to the middle where the purse was, then she let go of the rope and the giant fell in the water and drowned.

As for Kitty she ran back to the palace with the purse and the beautiful bedcover and gave them to the King, who married her as promised. They lived happy and they died happy and never drank out of a dry cappy.

THE RED ETIN

There once were two widows who lived in two cottages near to each other on the outskirts of Auchtermuchty. Each had a wee bit of land on which they grazed a cow and a few sheep to make a living. One had two sons and the other had one and these boys were the best of friends.

One day the eldest son of the widow with two sons decided to leave home and go out into the world to seek his fortune. The night before he left his mother told him to take a pan and go to the well for water and she would make him a bannock to take with him. 'But mind,' she said, 'the more water you bring, the bigger the bannock. It's all I have to give you.' But the pan had a hole in it and he only managed to bring home a wee bit of water, so she only made him a wee bannock. Small as it was though as she gave it to her son she asked him if he would have half of it with her blessing or the whole of it with her malison. The lad hesitated. It would have been good to leave with his mother's blessing but the bannock was wee and he had far to go and he didn't know when he would get more food so he took it all even though he had to listen to his mother's curse.

Before he left he took his younger brother aside and gave him his penknife, saying, 'Keep this beside you and look at it every morning. As long as the blade stays shiny and bright, then all is well with me. But if it should turn dull and rusty, then evil will have befallen me.'

The laddie set off and travelled until on the third day he came across an old shepherd sitting beside a flock of sheep. He asked, 'Who do these sheep belong to? Would your master maybe have a job for me?'

This was the answer he got:

> 'The Red Etin of Ireland
> Aince lived in Ballygan,
> And stole King Malcolm's daughter,
> The King of fair Scotland.
> He beats her, he binds her,
> He lays her on a band,
> And every day he dings her
> With a bright silver wand.
> Like Julian the Roman,
> He's one who fears no man.
> It's said there's one predestined
> To be his mortal foe,
> But that man is yet unborn,
> And lang may it be so.'

'That doesn't tell me much,' he thought, 'but I don't think I'd like him for a master.' So he went on his way.

He hadn't gone far though when he saw another old man with snow-white hair herding swine. Again he asked who the animals belonged to and if there would be a job as a swineherd. He got the same answer from the swineherd that he got from the shepherd.

'Curse that Red Etin. When will I be out of his domain?' he muttered to himself as he went on his way.

Presently he came across a very old man, so old he was quite bent with age. He was herding a flock of goats. Once more he asked who the animals belonged to and once more he got the same answer.

But this time the old goatherd added, 'Beware, stranger, of the next herd of beasts you meet. Sheep and swine and goats will harm no one but the creatures you meet next are like none you have seen before and they are not harmless.'

The young man thanked him and went on his way but he hadn't gone far when he came across a herd of very dreadful creatures the like of which he'd never dreamed.

Each had three heads and each head had four horns. When he saw them he was so afraid that he turned and ran off as fast and as far as he could until he was exhausted. He was just beginning to feel he could go no further when he saw a great castle in front of him, the door standing wide open.

He was so tired he walked straight in, and after wandering through some great halls which were quite deserted he came to the kitchen where an old woman was sitting by a fire.

He asked for a night's lodging and she agreed but added that he should be warned that this was the castle of the Red Etin, a monster with three heads who spared no one he could get hold of. Tired as he was the young man would have made his escape but he remembered the awful beasts outside. Afraid he might walk right into them in the growing dark, he begged the old woman to hide him somewhere and not tell the Red Etin he was in the castle. She agreed and hid him in a cupboard under the stairs. But just as he was falling asleep he heard an awful roaring and tramping above as the Red Etin arrived back.

'Seek but and seek ben,
I smell the smell of an earthly man,
Be he Frae Fife or be he Frae Tweed
His heart this night will kitchen my breid.'

The monster soon found the poor young man, and pulled him from his hiding place. When he was out he told him that if he could answer him three questions his life should be spared.

The first was: Whether Ireland or Scotland was first inhabited?

The second was: Whether man was made for woman, or woman for man?

The third was: Whether men or brutes were made first?

The lad not being able to answer any of these questions, the Red Etin took a mace and knocked him on the head, and turned him into a pillar of stone.

On the morning after this happened the younger brother took out the knife to look at it, and he was grieved to find it all brown with rust. He told his mother that the time was now come for him to go away upon his travels too; so she told him to take the can to the well for water, so she could bake a bannock for him. The can being broken, he brought home as little water as his brother had done, and the bannock was as small. She asked whether he would have the whole cake with her malison or the half with her blessing, and, like his brother, he thought it best to have the whole cake. So he went away, and everything happened to him that had happened to his brother!

The other widow and her son heard what had happened from a henwife and the young man determined that he would also go upon his travels and see if he could do anything to relieve his friends. So his mother gave him a can to go to the well and bring home water, so she could bake him a bannock for his journey. And he went and as he was bringing the water a

raven flew over his head and cried to him to look and he would
see that the water was running out. He was a young man of
sense, and seeing the water running out, he took some clay and
patched up the holes, so that he brought home enough water to
bake a large bannock. When his mother put it to him to take
half the bannock with her blessing, he took it in preference to
having the whole with her malison; and yet the half was bigger
than what the other lads had got all together.

So he went away on his journey; and after he had travelled a
fair way he met with an old woman, who asked him if he would
give her a bit of his bannock. And he said he would gladly do
that, and in return she gave him a magical hazel wand, which
she said might be of use to him if he took care to use it cor-
rectly. Then the old woman, who was a fairy, told him what
might happen to him, and what he ought to do, and then she
vanished. He went on his way, meeting the same herdsmen as
before, and when he asked whose beasts these were, the answer
this time was:

'The Red Etin of Ireland
Aince lived in Bellygan,
And stole King Malcolm's daughter,
The King of fair Scotland.
He beats her, he binds her,
He lays her on a band;
And every day he dings her
With a bright silver wand.
Like Julian the Roman,
He's one that fears no man,
But now I fear his end is near,
And destiny at hand;
And you're to be, I plainly see,
The heir of all his land.'

When he came to the place where the monstrous beasts were standing, he did not stop nor run away, but went boldly through among them. One came up roaring, mouth open ready to devour him so he struck it with his wand and in an instant it dropped dead at his feet. He soon came to the Red Etin's castle, where he knocked and was admitted. The old woman who sat by the fire warned him of the terrible Etin, and what had been the fate of the two brothers, but he was not to be daunted. The monster soon came in, saying:

'Snouk but and snouk ben,
I find the smell of an earthly man;
Be he living, or be he dead,
His heart shall be kitchen to my bread.'

He quickly spied the young man, and put the three questions to him, but the young man had been told everything by the good fairy so he was able to answer all the questions. When the Etin found this he knew that his power was gone. The young man then took up an axe and chopped off the monster's three heads. He next asked the old woman to show him where the King's daughter lay, and the old woman took him upstairs and opened a great many doors, and out of every door came a beautiful lassie who had been imprisoned there by the Etin; and one of the lassies was the King's daughter. She took him down into a low room, and there stood two stone pillars. He had only to touch them with his wand and his two friends and neighbours came back to life. All the prisoners were overjoyed at their rescue and thanked the young man. Next day they all set out for the King's court, and a fine procession they made. The King married his daughter to the young man who had rescued her, and gave a noble's daughter to the other two young men; and so they all lived happily all the rest of their days.

THE BLUE STANE

At the time St Regulus built the Four Knockit steeple at St Andrews there lived a giant at Blebocraigs. This giant was so angry at a building rising up in his view of the sea that he resolved to demolish it. Prising two huge blue-tinged boulders from the side of the nearby Drumcarrow Crag, he threw one at the tower. It didn't go very far at all, landing on a bank in what was in later years to become the garden of Mount Melville House. Then he borrowed his mother's apron to use as a sling to hurl a second boulder at the building. This went further but not far enough because in the act of throwing it the apron strings broke under the weight of the stone. It fell far short of its target and rested on a bank which is now the north-west corner of Alexandra Place.

The 'Blue Stane' in St Andrews became the stuff of legend. It was used for a long time as a meeting or trysting place, and was regarded with superstitious awe by passers-by. Men would give it a placatory pat and women a cautious curtsey as they passed by.

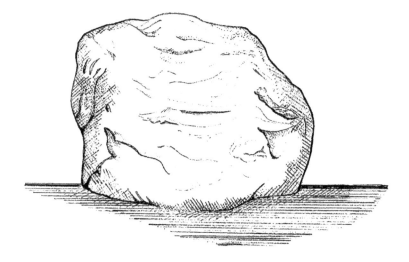

It is said that the pike men of St Andrews touched it for luck before departing in 1314 for the Battle of Bannockburn and they say it was used for the coronation of Kenneth McAlpine.

Most famously though, it was known as a gathering place for the fairy folk, in the days when fairy folk were blamed for all kinds of happenings. They were said to have been seen walking in procession to the stone from the fairy knoll near where the Martyrs Monument now stands. Two St Andrews worthies are said to have found out just how true this was.

One was Davie Duthie, a fisherman. He had a very bonnie wife. In fact, she was so bonnie that they say the fairies took a liking to her and stole her away. The poor man was distraught at her loss, especially since he heard her every morning singing softly to him from above his bed. He couldn't see her, just hear the plaintive song.

One day he was stacking creels at the harbour when he happened to stand on one leg as hens do in rainy weather. The enchantment which held his wife in fairyland was immediately broken and to his surprise there she was standing in front of him.

The fisherman had a brother in his misfortune, a drunken ploughman from Strathkinness. His wife was continually nagging him about his bad behaviour but everything she said fell on him like rain on the desert and had no effect.

Because she felt she couldn't be happy with him she was driven to visit the Blue Stane and say that she wished the fairies would come and take her away. No sooner were the words out than the fairies took hold of her and in a twinkling she was whisked up in the air as they sang:

> 'Deedle linkum, deedum ness,
> We're aff wi' drunken Archie's wife,
> The Plooman O' Strathkinness.'

They carried her off to Cauldhame – the palace of the fairies – where she lived like a queen. But blood they say is thicker than water and she began to miss her husband so she asked to be returned to him. This was granted and as she left the fairies one of them presented her with a small stick saying, 'As long as you keep this your gudeman will drink no more.' The charm was successful. Archie became a sober man and the gudewife never forgot the kindness of the fairies.

THE WHITE STAG OF STRATHTYRUM

According to legend a white stag roams the woods on Strathtyrum Estate near St Andrews and if you are lucky enough to meet him he might whisk you off to meet the fairies who live in the fairy knowe on Kinninmonth Hill. My grandfather worked on the estate and lived in a cottage in the woods. He told me this story.

There once was a wee girl staying with her grannie who lived in a cottage in the woods. It was the first time she had stayed there so she was really excited and a wee bit scared because she had been brought up on fairy tales so she knew that sometimes things happened to folk who stayed in houses in the wood.

Through the night she heard noises so she got up to look out of the window. That's when she saw it.

She knew it was a deer because she had seen pictures but she'd not seen one like this before. It was pure white and it seemed to be looking straight at her. So she pushed her feet into her baffies, threw on her jacket and slipped out the kitchen door. There it stood, almost shining in the moonlight. She stretched out her hand to stroke it and before she knew what was happening she was up on its back and they were flying through the woods, over the burn, over the top of Drumcarrow Crag till it set her down on the slopes of Kinninmonth Hill.

She looked around, wondering what to do next. Then she saw a wee door on the hillside open and a wee wifie, dressed in a green frock with a white apron, came out. 'Oh dear,' she thought, 'a fairy wife.'

The fairy wife beckoned to her and said, 'Come awa in if yer coming, lassie.'

She followed her into the hill, down a long passage until they came to a big hall, full of fairy folk. They seemed to be having a party. There was music playing and they were heuching and teuching, whirling and birling all around. The girl sat down to watch and after a while the music stopped and the fairy folk sat down for a cup of tea. A fairy wife offered her a cup and a cake but she said 'No.' She remembered her granny telling her never to take food or drink from a fairy because you'd be forever in their power.

After the tea was finished a fairy man stood up. The girl thought it must be the Fairy King because he had a wee crown on his head.

'It's time for the turns!' he announced. Then a wee lassie stood up and sang a really braw song. Then a wee man played a tune on a fiddle and another played on a whistle. After that there was silence. Everybody seemed to be looking at her. The Fairy King stood up and said, 'Come on lassie, if ye come tae wan o' oor pairties ye hae tae dae a turn before ye can gan hame.'

Oh no! She didn't know what to do. She'd never learned to play an instrument and even her mother said she couldn't sing for toffee. Then she had an idea; she knew her fairy tales so she would tell them a story and she did. Well they roared and laughed and clapped so she asked if she could go home now. They said 'Aye' so she followed the fairy wife out onto the hill where the white deer was waiting. She climbed on its back and in a wink of an eye she was back in her bedroom looking out the of window, just in time to see a flash of white disappearing into the trees.

Now, the girl didn't know if it had really happened or if it had all been a dream but she did know that she got told off the next day for having mud on her baffies.

The Strathmiglo Broonie

In days gone by there was said to be a Broonie who stayed in the castle of the Baron of Strathmiglo. Every day the Broonie would travel to the neighbouring Cash Farm. The route took him over the fields, through the woods and across the Miglo Burn. In these days there was no bridge at the east mill so he crossed by way of the stepping stones.

At the farm he laboured cheerfully as these small industrious yet sometimes irritable people always did. He laboured in the barn and the byre, threshing the corn or milking the cows for the poor neighbours of the lordly baron in whose castle he stayed. Folk couldn't see the Broonie, no mortal eyes could, but everybody could see the results of his work. And what did he want in return? Nothing except the leave to eat from any dish he chose as long as it hadn't been specially set aside for him. To offer any direct reward or bribe to a Broonie for his services would, as all those versed in fairy lore know, cause the loss of his valuable service for ever.

Folk would be sitting down to their porridge and half would disappear before their eyes. Then somebody might sit down to their dinner and again half would disappear. But nobody minded because his help was always welcome.

One morning, after a night of particularly heavy rain, the Miglo Burn flooded and the stepping stones were completely covered. The nearest bridge was miles away at the west end of the town so the folk at the farm didn't expect the Broonie would come. 'The Broonie will no be here the day,' they were

heard to say, 'he'll no go round as far as the bridge. We'll have to do all the work oorsel the day.'

But the Broonie had different ideas. He'd been more anxious to serve the farmer than they supposed and he hadn't been so easily put off performing his usual tasks. One of the maids had just sat down to enjoy her morning porridge and hadn't taken any more than a couple of spoonfuls when she found the Broonie was really there because the contents of the bowl made a speedy disappearance without any help from her. 'How did you get over the water?' she blurted out. To everyone's amazement a deep gruff voice was heard to say, 'I came round by the brig.'

From that day on the locals were heard to say, 'Gae roond by the brig like the Broonie did,' if someone took the long way round.

THE BOGHALL BROONIE

'There were aucht sturdy ploomen
On the farm o' Bogha';
But Broonie in ae nicht,
Wrought mair than them a'.'

The Broonie was very like a man in shape but his body was covered in brown hair, hence the name. He was very strong, slept all day and worked all night while the rest of the farm-house was asleep. He was harmless and had a more forgiving than revengeful nature. The only reward he would take for his trouble was to be fed on sowans and sweet milk and to have a bed of straw in a cosy corner of the barn.

To the farm at Boghall near Kingsbarns the Broonie was essential. As the local rhyme said, he did more work in one night than all the other workers did in a day. But one very severe winter, when the snow lay deep on the ground and the frost was so intense as to freeze every running burn and well, the gude-wife, afraid that her friend the Broonie would die of cold out in the barn, and quite ignorant that she was doing wrong, spread some warm blankets on his straw bed. When he saw them he immediately left the farm, saying:

'To leave my old haunts, oh! my heart is sair,
But the wife gae me blankets – she'll see me nae mair;
I've worked in her barn, frae evening till day,
My curse on the blankets that drove me away,
All the boon that I asked were my sowans and strae,
But success to Bogha' although Broonie's away.'

They say Boghall Farm has never been the same since.

CAPTIVE IN FAIRYLAND

Sir Alan Mortimer, Lord of Aberdour, had a daughter, Emma. From the day she was born he doted on her. He watched over her, would do anything for her, nothing was too good, nothing refused. She was said to be a bonnie lassie, eyes as bright as gems, hair as black as jet.

She fell in love with a young knight, Lord Bethune. When he rode off to fight in Palestine, she was broken-hearted but her father built her a retreat, formed from woodbine and jasmine, and every day until twilight, Emma would retire there to dream of her brave knight. It is said she would stay there until the setting sun had ceased to bathe St Columba's Tower with golden light and the evening star was shining in the night sky.

One day Sir Alan had been entertaining in his castle, little knowing that the laughter and merriment would by nightfall have turned to sadness and terror. He didn't know that as the

moon rose that evening the fairy folk would be out having their own great celebration. The Fairy King himself had chosen this very evening to convene his court and take the opportunity to pick through his beauties to choose a Fairy Queen.

The evening star had just begun to glow when Emma left her bower to return home. At that same moment the fairy folk had gathered and fairy music began to play. The Fairy King spotted the beautiful Emma and instantly fell in love with her. No other would do. He would have this beauty for his Fairy Queen.

Taking on the form of Emma's beloved Lord Bethune, he approached his chosen one. Believing her lover had at last returned, she rushed into the arms of the Fairy King, and vanished from human sight.

The abbey bell had rung the evening hour when Sir Alan noticed that Emma had not returned. Gathering servants and hounds around him, he rushed out into the night to search for her. But the hounds all lay down on the heather and howled. Sir Alan was at their head but when he heard the hounds yowl he tore his hair. He cheered his servants on but his heart was breaking. 'Unearthly sounds affright my hounds. Unearthly sights they see. I fear the fairies have stolen my daughter. Hurry to the holy abbot on Inchcolm. Tell him a son of the Kirk implores his aid.'

A boat was sent to the Abbot of Inchcolm himself, where messengers pleaded with him to put on his spiritual armour and help the beautiful Emma.

The abbot returned in the boat with the servants and, grasping the baron's hand, told him, 'Have patience son, for I shall expel the fiends o' hell frae you castle and Barony.'

'Give me back my daughter,' replied the baron, 'and this very night I will give half my gold to St Columba's shrine, and half my lands to the abbey.'

'Have patience sir. No fiend has withstood me yet when I have brandished the holy cross. I give my word that your daughter shall be back with you before I sleep tonight. Did I not make a pilgrimage to Palestine barefoot? Have I not slept at the Holy Sepulchre and seen visions? Have I not bathed seven times in Siloam's sacred stream? And did not holy St Bride hang a crucifix around my neck in a dream? On this rosary there is a bead which has cured three men bewitched and a relic of the real cross adorns my pastoral staff.'

Carrying a chalice in his hand, full to the brim of clear water that had oozed from the roof of the Holy Sepulchre, the abbot sprinkled Sir Alan's lands with the water and the fairies with a yell flew off into the darkness. He took his rosary and invoked St Mary's name until Emma's voice could be heard chanting a hymn. When he brandished the holy cross and raised it to the sky she burst into their sight.

Sir Alan was overjoyed and did indeed bequeath gold and land to the Church.

2

GHOSTS AND VISIONS

JENNY NETTLES

Jenny Nettles, a native of Strathmiglo, was a bonnie lassie, as innocent as the day is long. She attracted the attention of a Highland officer who was attached to Rob Roy's command when they were garrisoned at Falkland Palace. They met frequently amongst the trees between Falkland and Strathmiglo. Trusting him, she fell in love, succumbing to his charms and promises of marriage. But the promises were broken. She heard the garrison was moving back to the Highlands and he was going with them, alone.

She went to the palace, bringing with her their newborn child, hoping to seek out her lover and implore him to keep his promise and take them with him, thinking that love and pity would melt his callous heart.

She waited at the gates, eagerly watching and at last he appeared amongst a crowd of comrades who noticed the young lass and cast her admiring glances, but she had eyes only for her lover. She threw herself weeping at his feet, only to be thrust aside with muttered revenge.

Distraught, she wandered for days in the countryside, refusing to respond to offers of food and shelter and when kindly folk tried to steer her and her child to safety she ran off, never to be seen alive again.

Eventually the infant was found, dead on a mossy bank below a spreading tree from which the mother had hanged herself. She was buried in that place and it is said she wanders still in the night, the infant in her arms. Travellers coming upon the grave at night have seen a vivid light shine on the grave and a female form gazing down on a golden cradle singing sweet lullabies to a child.

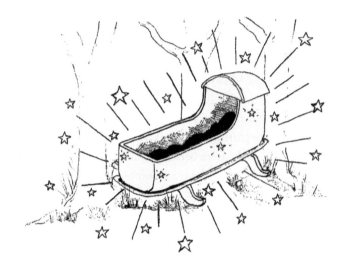

THE GHOST OF PITFIRRANE

A long, long time ago the folk of Pitfirrane Estate near Dunfermline were sorely troubled by a ghost who appeared every night, dressed in a shroud as if newly risen from his grave. It would be heard wailing and moaning as it rattled doors, looked through windows and circled the old elm tree while chanting these words:

'Frae the auld elm tree, on tap o' the knowe,
A seed shall fa' aff whilk a tree shall grow;
And a cradle it shall mak', to rock the wee bairn,
Wha'll conjure the ghaist that haunts Pitfirrane.'

The folk of the estate were too afraid to go out at night and kept themselves behind closed doors in the hours of darkness. Well most of them were too afraid; Tam, the carpenter, was not. He was a good man, making the bonniest things from wood, but he also had a sharp mind and some said he had the second sight. He listened to the chanting of the poor demented soul and pondered the words as he worked. At last it came to him what he had to do. You see there was an identical elm tree near the haunted one, not so old but a strong healthy tree nevertheless. The carpenter cut down this tree and kept the trunk in his yard for a long time until one day he was asked to make a cradle. Of course he had to make it from the elm.

The bairn, William, who filled the cradle, grew up to be a very clever laddie, so much so that the minister and the teacher had words with the laird and money was found to send him to St Andrews University to study for the Church.

When he returned home to Pitfirrane the carpenter, now a very old man, told the young cleric the story and that he thought William was the one to lay the ghost to rest.

Arming himself with book and candle the young man visited the haunted tree and on the appearance of the ghost, asked what help he could be. The dead soul confessed to having committed a murder in his lifetime and told the cleric to dig amongst the roots of the old elm where the bones of the victim would be found. This done, the bones were given a proper burial in the churchyard and the ghost was never seen nor heard again.

THE VANISHING VILLAGE

On the uplands which rise from the coast between Anstruther and St Andrews and behind Crail and Kingsbarns stretch what was once the great wasteland of the King's Muir. Beyond the Kenly Burn and in the vicinity of the cathedral city its name changes to the Pryor's Muir. In times gone by these formed the 'Muirs of Fife'.

These Muirs have many a tale to tell for those who have ears to listen.

Weirdest of all the parishes which now divide the Muirs between them is that of Dunino. Here the Lathockar burn meets with the Cameron Burn and cuts its way through a dark wooded gorge bending round the height on which stand the kirk and the manse and which rises to the dun itself at the north east. Fragments of druid stones bear testimony to long forgotten faiths and rites. In the den itself, the Bell Crag rises up with its curious pothole at the summit, believed by some to be a place of sacrifice, the blood of the victim being caught in the cavity. Marks on the stone are said to have been made by the Arch Druid sharpening his knife and the two hollows where he planted his feet. It is still believed that wishes made there will be fulfilled and that the spirits of the druids are still able to bewitch those strangers who venture alone into their once sacred grove, as this curious tale shows.

Some years ago when many of the roads in this part of Fife were rarely used, a visitor to the district chanced to ride this way while travelling from the south coast to St Andrews. He had heard of Dunino Kirk and knew something of its associations so he decided to make a detour and visit it. He followed the rough track leading down to the bridge across the Pitmilly Burn. From there he followed the well-made path cut into the hillside to climb through the trees to the kirk itself. Continuing on the level track round the side of the hill he saw on the far side of the burn in front of him a picturesque hamlet. Some of the cottages were thatched, some tiled, but all were covered with roses and creepers. In front, strips of garden stretching to the burn were trimly kept and full of flowers. Behind, the gardens took on more the nature of a kailyard. At the east end, on slightly higher ground, stood a smiddy. No sound broke the stillness of the summer afternoon except the murmuring of the burn. At one or two of the doors stood old men in knee breeches and broad bonnets and old women in white mutches and stiff gowns, while in the entrance to the smiddy the smith leant motionless on his hammer. It was as though life's nurse in nurse's fashion had lulled the world to sleep.

Lulled into a half dream-like state by the peace and stillness, the visitor turned and climbed back to the church and because time was short, when he had viewed the church, he did not return that way. No sense of the abnormal occurred to him and he met no one until he returned to the main road. A year or more passed before the traveller returned to the area. It was autumn and shades of gold and russet could be seen in the surrounding woodlands. This time he was accompanied by a companion to whom he had told the story of his glimpse of 'the most old-world hamlet in Fife'. They took the same pathway as before, crossing the bridge, and got ready to see what the traveller had described. But the cottages were gone! The burn flowed as he had last seen it but the opposite bank was bare. The traveller could but assure his companion of the truth of his vision and leave the riddle to be solved by other minds.

THE VEILED NUN OF ST LEONARDS

In the days of Mary Queen of Scots, there lived in South Street, St Andrews, a very lovely young lady who belonged to a very old local family. It is said her beauty and wit brought many admirers to claim her hand but with little success as she turned them all away. At last though she did fall in love and became engaged to a handsome young man from East Lothian, a student at the university, and for many months all went well and wedding plans were well underway. But the course of true love doesn't always run smoothly and clouds began to appear on the horizon. The young man got cold feet and, deciding marriage wasn't for him, headed back to his family of the other side of the Forth.

The young lady was devastated and declared she would never be an earthly bride but would take the veil and become a bride of the Church, a nun. Her family tried to dissuade her, but she was determined and immediately left home. They sent word to the young man in the hope that he would help. On hearing that she had left home and entered a nunnery he at once announced that he would immediately leave for St Andrews, seize her and marry her at once, much to the joy of her parents.

He did return to St Andrews almost immediately but he was to receive a terrible shock when he got there. On meeting his once beautiful fiancé he discovered that not only had she become a nun but rather than ever become an earthly bride she had also mutilated her face by slitting her nostrils, cutting off her eyelids and both her top and bottom lips, and had branded her fair cheeks with hot irons.

The poor young man, on seeing her former beauty destroyed fled to Edinburgh, where he committed suicide. And the young girl, having become a nun, died from grief and remorse.

Now all that happened over 400 years ago but her ghost, with its marred and mutilated face, still wanders the path from

St Leonard's kirk gate to the Pends, known today as Nun's Walk. She is all dressed in black with a long black veil over her face and she carries a lantern in her hand. Should anyone meet her in the lane, she slowly sweeps aside her veil and raises the lantern to reveal her awful features. It is also said that if you do have the misfortune to look on her scarred face you won't have long for this world as I was told, much later but still many years ago, by the head gardener at St Leonards School, one George England. The story goes that a student friend of his had invited a cousin from London to come and stay in St Andrews for some golf. They came to visit George at home one evening, his home being a few yards from the end of Nun's Walk. During the visit, one of the men decided to step outside for a smoke and to take in some night air. It was quite late when the other left but a few minutes later he returned, hammering on the door and asking for help. He had found his cousin slumped against a tree on Nun's Walk. He had approached him but the poor man had looked on him with horror, saying, 'Oh no! Have you come to me again?' and immediately fainted.

George and his friend took him to his rooms and stayed with him till he came round. He told them that he had wandered up the pends and on seeing the wee lane decided to explore it. About half way along he noticed a light coming towards him. Thinking it was a policeman he approached, wishing the figure a good evening. He got no reply but as the figure drew nearer he realised it was a veiled woman with a lantern. She came up quite close, stopped and drew back her veil and held up the lantern. 'I can never forget nor describe that horrible fearful face,' he said. 'I dropped like a stone at her feet and remember no more till I found myself here with you at my side. I will leave here tomorrow on the first train.' And he did. George and his friend never saw him again, but six months later the student received a letter telling him his cousin had been visited by the same awful spectre in his rooms in London and exactly a year later he had word of his death from heart failure and he wondered if once again he had been visited by the veiled nun of St Leonards.

THE MINSTREL OF BALCOMIE

Around the time of the Battle of Flodden in 1513, the Laird of Balcomie Castle, near Crail, had in his service a young laddie called Jack. Jack was a hard-working, well-liked wee laddie who just loved music. He liked to listen to the pipers and the fiddlers and the box players when they came to the castle to entertain the laird. He didn't only listen though, he liked to play as well and what he liked to play was his penny whistle, which his grandad had taught him when he was quite young. As soon as he woke up in the morning he began to play. He played on the way to the kitchen where he was supposed to help the cook. He played when he went to fetch the water. He played when he took the swill to the pigs. In fact he played all day long from the minute he woke up until he went to bed at night. Most of the time the folk in the castle didn't mind because after all he was good and the airs he played were tuneful and cheery.

One time the laird had a big party. The folk in the castle had been up most of the night dancing and eating and drinking. So the laird wasn't right pleased when he was wakened up in the early morning when Jack began to play while pacing the corridor where his master was asleep after his night of celebration and entertaining. The laird really just wanted to be left alone to sleep in peace. In fact, he was so annoyed at being disturbed that he rushed from his room, grabbed the poor lad by the throat, picked him up, took him downstairs and threw him in the deepest dungeon under the castle keep where he locked him in and then went back to bed, meaning to let him out again at a more civilised hour.

When the laird eventually woke up again, because of the excesses of the evening before, he completely forgot about the servant boy. He set off with his servants to Edinburgh. It wasn't till his return seven days later when he heard the boy was missing and everyone was looking for him that he remembered the incident. Rushing to the dungeon he found his worst fears confirmed: the boy had starved to death.

From that day on, it is said, a figure which looks like a young boy has been seen flitting along the castle corridors and up and down the stairs where the laddie used to wander, and on winter nights when the stars are sharp and clear and the moon is on the wane, it is said he wanders beyond the confines of the castle. At such times wild bursts of unearthly whistling comes from the darkness of the keep and the auld fishermen of Crail often report seeing him sitting on top of the castle flagpole, a rusty penny whistle at his lips.

THE LEGEND OF GREEN JEAN

Green Jean or Green Jeannie seems to be a very popular name for ghosts in Fife, several castles and big houses laying claim to such an apparition. The two stories I have recorded here were told to me by an elderly relative and by a lady I met in hospital.

Just to the west of West Wemyss lies Wemyss Castle, reported to be haunted by one 'Green Jean'. Her restless spirit wanders through certain rooms in the castle, a beautiful lady, tall and slim, dressed in a trailing gown of green that swishes as she glides. Who she is isn't known as those who would, keep her secret well. The story of one sighting was told by Millicent, wife of Mr Hay Erskine Wemyss, resident and at that time owner of the castle.

One Christmas they were having a large party of guests to stay with them. For the amusement of her guests Millicent had arranged to put on a small play on Christmas night. She had taken the carriage and driven to Kirkcaldy, the nearest town in those days, to get some things she still needed for the night's entertainment.

Everything was prepared for the play, which was to take place in the large room used as a dining room. A stage had been erected at one end and a curtain hung in readiness. There was a small room leading from the stage, its door in front of the curtain, and in full view. Although empty at the time, the room was sometimes used by the butler to store glasses, but the door was always kept locked.

On the afternoon in question two girls, Millicent's eldest daughter and her friend, were sitting by the fire. It was a cold, wet afternoon and although it was late, there was no light except for the fire roaring in the huge fireplace. The doors were shut but no candles had been lit. Apart from the sound of the two girls chatting about the forthcoming entertainment, and the heavy rain battering against the window, no other noise could be heard. Suddenly a rustling sound reached their ears, coming from the stage. They looked up, the curtain was still down but slowly it was gently pushed aside to make room for the entry of a tall, pale lady dressed in green who held a lit Egyptian-looking lamp. The lady took no notice of the girls but, holding the lamp well in front of her, walked calmly, her long gown swishing as she went, up to the locked door, opened it, passed into the room and closed it noiselessly behind her. The girls, much excited, rushed to the door. Millicent's daughter shouted to her friend, 'Fetch a candle,' as there was no other way out of the room. A candle was quickly lit and the door unlocked but the room was pitch dark and there was no sign of the Green Lady; she had disappeared into space.

At the sound of Millicent's carriage returning the girls rushed out to meet her, shouting, 'We've seen Green Jean.' Millicent was not herself bothered about such things but being a bit concerned what effect such a tale would have on her guests and servants and not wanting to spoil the forthcoming festivities, she hushed the story up at the time.

Not long afterwards, however, she saw the Green Lady herself. Her sitting room, where she always sat to write her letters, overlooked the sea just a stone's throw away. The door opened onto a long gallery, onto which several other doors opened. The room next door was her son's sitting room, which he used for business and which overlooked a small courtyard with a small patch of grass in the middle. One evening, a pouring wet night, Millicent's son had not returned after being out riding most of the day. His mother was anxious that he should come home as he had a rather weak chest. Suddenly she heard the doorbell ring followed by her son's hasty footsteps enter his sitting room and then his bedroom. Feeling relieved, but knowing he would not be pleased to think she had been spying on him, even if she was just concerned for his health, she waited quietly in her sitting room. After about half an hour, hearing no more movement, she popped her head into his sitting room and into his bedroom. Seeing his wet clothes were lying on the floor in a heap she was satisfied and passed once again into the gallery. Much to her surprise she saw, coming towards her along the corridor, a tall lady dressed in green. She couldn't for a minute think who this might be as it was someone she had never seen before. The lady walked in a slow dignified way, completely undisturbed by meeting someone else in the corridor. For a moment Millicent just stared in astonishment, then in a flash she realised who this was. 'It's Green Jean,' she said to herself. 'I'll wait till she comes alongside and see what she says.' She waited. Green Jean drew alongside her but turned her head away. Millicent walked with her to the end of the corridor, wanting to speak but unable to find the words. Then, in a blink of an eye, Green Jean disappeared! Afterwards, Millicent wished she had had the courage to ask who she was.

Another 'Green Jean' is said to frequent a gateway on the Newburgh to Auchtermuchty road at an old house called Pitcairlie. The story goes that Jean, daughter of the Laird of Pitcairlie, fell in love with one of their young footmen and they used to meet by this gate. When her father found out he was furious and, confronting the footman in the room at the top of the tower, stabbed him to death in a rage. His daughter, witnessing the assault, was so distraught that she threw herself off the battlements. Her spirit, they say, dressed in a long green dress, continues to wait by the gate for her lover. To this day the locals of Auchtermuchty tell each other this story and the sharp bend in the road just past the gate is known to them as Jeannie's bend. There are frequent accidents on this bit of road and folk say, 'Aye, it must have been Jeannie again.'

THE MIDNIGHT BURIAL

By the light of candle and lamp round the hearths of Auchtertool, it is whispered that every year on the same night in August a ghostly procession comes along the 'Lady's Walk' to the kirk, bearing a shrouded coffin shoulder-high and led by a piper, clad in the tartan of the Skene family, playing an ancient lament. The story tells that a Jacobite, a Skene of Halyards, died in exile in France. His body was brought home to Fife from France for burial in the Skene family vault in the then ruined aisle of the Kirk of Auchtertool. By then the Skenes, ruined through adherence to the Jacobite cause, had sold the family home, the great mansion or 'Palace of Halyards', to the Earl of Moray. It was with the earl's permission that the dead Skene's body rested in Halyards before burial, and it was from there at the 'kirk midnight' that Skene's funeral procession made its way by torchlight, accompanied by old family friends and servants by way of the 'Lady's Walk' and the fields straight across to the Kirk of Auchtertool. All was done according to Skene family tradition in the matter of burials and the dead Skene was interred in the family vault in the warm darkness of a high summer night. He was buried, however, according to the rites of the Roman Catholic Church, for in France he had been converted to the faith of the Stuarts. Buried by torchlight in the Skene vault where by the late nineteenth century, according to the then minister of Auchtertool Kirk, even the 'auld banes, wi a handle o' silks an' ribbons' seen earlier in the century by the Auchtertool sexton had 'vanished' or turned to dust.

The old ghostly tale does not say on which night in August the unearthly funeral is supposed to take place but they do say that as a boy Sir Walter Scot was present at the weird Skene funeral and based an account of a funeral in one of his works on this strange internment.

The Boy in the Cupboard

One wild December day the lady of a certain house in Burntisland was alone for the first time. She hadn't been long married and had just moved in to the big old house about half a mile from the coast. Her husband had gone to Dunfermline on business and the servants were all out for various reasons. After an extra furious gust of wind, she was startled by a noise at the door. On opening it she was shocked to see four unknown men dressed like sailors march in without a word, apparently carrying the lifeless body of a young lad. They carried him upstairs to a small bedroom at the back of the house. They stopped beside a large cupboard which occupied one side of the room, and while two men held the boy, the other two moved a small camp-bed which was nearby and laid the boy on it gently. Then all four marched out. All this time she watched, dumb with astonishment.

A few minutes after the men left a beautiful young lady ran into the room. She was dressed in old-fashioned clothes of rich and elaborate material. The woman was startled to hear the girl shout at the boy, who seemed to have recovered his senses. She stepped forward to ask what was happening and to her horror found she could see the boy's face through the body of the girl. With great difficulty she kept her composure and seated herself in the corner to watch what was to unfold.

'Jack, Jack!' the young girl called. 'He is coming. Hide yourself. He is within a hundred yards of the house.'

'I cannot, Agnes,' the boy replied, with a look of terror and fatigue. 'I'm too weak and there is nowhere to hide.'

'Hide in here,' she said, quickly opening the cupboard and, pressing a spring at the back, revealing a dark opening. 'Quick now my poor boy,' she said tenderly, helping the boy at the same time.

She had just time to close the spring door and the door of the cupboard when the door of the room was opened violently and a tall, stern-looking black-bearded man strode in.

'Where is the boy?' he shouted. Receiving no answer he took a small dagger from his belt and repeated his question. This time the girl firmly refused to give information so without hesitation he plunged the dagger into her heart. Instantly all vanished but before the lady of the house could compose herself she heard scratching coming from the cupboard and agonising cries of despair. She tried to rise and go to the cupboard but found she couldn't move.

The next thing she knew she was waking up with her husband standing over her, She told him the whole story and together they searched the cupboard. After much searching they found the spring and on opening the door they found a few mouldering bones and a large but illegible manuscript. The whole thing was treated as a dream until a caretaker was horrified to find he was chosen to be the next spectator of the tragedy, after which the house was pulled down and the site covered with wheat crops.

3

Nurses' Tales

These are some of the stories of my childhood. Although they may have been told in other parts of Scotland they were certainly being told in Fife in the nineteenth century, in the days of my great-grandparents, because they told them to my grandparents and my mother and they in turn told them to me. I've called them nurses' tales because many of the better-off families would have had a nurse or nanny to look after the children and these nurses would tell stories and sing ballads. One such nurse in particular is mentioned by collectors as a source, a certain Jeannie Durie from Rossie in Fife.

The Well at the World's End

Once upon a time there was a King and a Queen and they each had a daughter. The King's daughter was bonnie and good tempered and everyone liked her, but the Queen's daughter was ugly and bad tempered, so nobody liked her. Over time, the Queen grew jealous of the King's daughter so she decided to get rid of her. One day, when the King was away, she gave the girl a bottle and asked her to go to the Well at the World's End and fetch some of the clear sparkling water to be found there, hoping that she would get lost and not return.

The girl took the bottle and away she went. Far and far she travelled till she came to a field of sharp thorns. She was just wondering how she would get across when she noticed a horse tethered nearby and the horse said to her:

> 'Free me, free me,
> My bonnie maiden,
> For I've no been free
> Seven years and a day!'

'Yes I'll free you,' said the King's daughter, and she did.

'Jump on my back and I'll carry you over the field of sharp thorns,' said the horse. So she did and the horse carried her over the field and set her down on the other side.

The girl travelled on far and far and farther than I can tell until at last she came to the Well at the World's End. But she found the well was very deep and she couldn't reach the water. She was just thinking what to do when up popped three scaly men's heads. They looked up at her and said:

> 'Wash me, wash me,
> My bonnie maiden,
> And dry me with
> Your clean linen apron!'

'Yes I'll wash you,' said the King's daughter. She washed the heads and dried them with her clean linen apron. They took the bottle and dipped it and filled it with clear sparkling water. Then they said, one to another:

'Wish, Brother Wish! What will you wish?'

'I wish,' said the first, 'that if she is bonnie now then may she be ten times bonnier by the time she gets home.'

'Aye,' said the second, 'I wish that every time she speaks, a precious diamond falls from her mouth.'

'And I wish,' said the third, 'that every time she combs her hair, a peck of gold and silver falls to the ground.'

So the King's daughter took the bottle and travelled home. When the Queen saw her she was furious. Not only had she found her way there and back but now she was ten times bonnier than she had been before and every time she spoke precious jewels fell from her mouth and every time she brushed her hair gold and silver fell to the ground.

Then the Queen thought that if the King's daughter could be so lucky then her daughter could too. So she gave her own daughter a bottle and sent her to the Well at the World's End.

The girl took the bottle and travelled till she came to the field of sharp thorns. She was just wondering how she would get across when she noticed the horse tethered nearby and the horse said:

'Free me, free me,
My bonny maiden,
For I've no been free
Seven years and a day.'

'Do you not know I'm the Queen's daughter?' said the girl. 'I'm not going to waste my time and dirty my hands by freeing a silly old horse like you!'

'Then I'll not carry you over the field of sharp thorns,' said the horse.

So the girl had to walk over the field and the thorns cut her till she could hardly walk. But she travelled on until she too came to the Well at the World's End. But the well was so deep that she couldn't reach the water to fill the bottle. As she sat there wondering what to do, three scaly men's heads looked up at her and said:

'Wash me, wash me,
Young maiden,
And dry me with
Your clean linen apron!'

'What! Do you think I'm going to wash the likes of you?' she said. 'Do you not know I'm the Queen's daughter?' She didn't wash their heads, so they didn't fill the bottle.

Then they said to one another, 'Wish, Brother Wish! What will you wish?'

'I wish,' said the first, 'that if she is ugly now then may she be ten times uglier by the time she gets home.'

'Aye,' said the second, 'I wish that every time she speaks, frogs and toads fall from her mouth.'

'And I wish,' said the third, 'that every time she combs her hair a peck of fleas and lice fall to the ground.'

So the Queen's daughter took the empty bottle and travelled home. When the Queen saw her she was mad with rage. Not only was she ten times uglier than she had been before, but every time she spoke frogs and toads fell from her mouth and every time she combed her hair fleas and lice fell to the ground. The Queen was so ashamed of her daughter that she sent her away. So when a handsome prince came by looking for a wife he married the King's daughter.

JOCK AND HIS LULLS

There once was a woman living in the Kingdom of Fife who had two sons, both called Jock. The laddies were good to their mother, helping about the house and looking after the few cattle they had.

One day the elder of the two said, 'Mother, it's time I went to make my own way in the world and seek my own fortune, whatever that may be.'

Now the woman was sad that her son wanted to leave but she understood that this was the way of things. So she sent him to the well for water so she could make him a bannock for the journey. She gave him a cracked dish and a sieve and told him that the more water he brought back, the bigger the bannock she would be able to make. So Jock set off for the well and there, sitting on a rock was a wee bird. As Jock approached the bird piped up:

'Stuff it with moss and clag it with clay and that will carry the water away.'

But Jock thought there was no way he was letting a bird tell him what to do so he took the water home in the cracked dish but there was only a wee drop left for his mother and so she just baked him a wee bannock. He put the bannock in his pocket and set off on his journey to seek his fortune.

He had been walking for an hour or two when he decided to sit down to eat his bannock. A wee bird, the same wee bird from before, came and landed beside him.

'If you give me a bit of your bannock, I'll give you a feather from my wing to make lulls,' said the bird.

'Away with you,' said Jock. 'I've hardly enough to feed myself never mind give you a bit. Now shoo.'

Well the wee bird flew away and Jock walked on till he came to a big house. 'Maybe I can get some work here,' he thought. So he went up to the house and knocked on the door. After a while it was opened by an old woman. 'What do you want?' she asked.

'I'm looking for work. Is there any going?'

'And what kind of work can you do?'

'Well,' said Jock, 'I can carry ashes, wash dishes, dig the garden and herd cattle.'

'Herd cattle, can you? How do you think you would do herding hares?'

'I think I could manage that,' said Jock, thinking it sounded a bit strange.

'Well then,' said the woman, 'if you can go down to the field and take care of the hares and bring them all home tonight, you'll get to marry the daughter of the house.'

Jock thought that sounded fine. He was sure he could manage some hares and if he married the daughter he would have made his fortune no bother. So he went down to the field where there were twenty-four hares all running about and one lame one sitting by itself. Jock thought that this was going to be easy as he sat down on a rock by the gate to watch the hares. But after a while he started to feel a bit hungry. All he'd had to eat all day had been the wee bannock his mum had made. As his stomach began to rumble he thought to himself that no one would miss the lame hare, so he grabbed it, snapped its neck and set a fire to roast it. It didn't take long but he was so busy thinking about himself that he didn't notice the other hares had been watching him and now they had all disappeared into the walls and hedges to hide. When nightfall came Jock searched the field and all the other fields but not one hare could he find. So he returned to the house and when the folk there saw he hadn't brought back any hares they hanged him.

Meanwhile, back at the farm the second son was thinking it was time he too went out into the world to seek his fortune. Now the woman was even sadder that this son wanted to leave her all on her own. But she understood this was the way of things. So she sent him to the well for water so she could make a bannock for the journey. She gave him the same dish and sieve and told him the more water he brought back the bigger the bannock he would get. So he set off for the well and when he got there the wee bird was waiting for him. It piped up:

'Stuff it with moss and clag it with clay and that will carry the water away.'

'Thank you,' he said, 'that's a good idea, I'll do that.'

So he lined the sieve and dish with moss and clay and took a full sieve and a full dish back to his mother so she made him a fine big bannock. The next day he put the bannock in his pocket and set off. It wasn't long till he began to feel hungry so he sat down to eat his bannock. He had just broken a bit off when the wee bird appeared. 'That's a fine big bannock you have there. If you give me a bit I'll give you a feather from my wing to make lulls with.'

Jock thought that sounded a good trick so he gave the bird a bit of bannock and it let him pull a feather from its wing and it turned into a great set of pipes right before his eyes. Jock was delighted and he set off on his journey again playing himself a tune as he went, till he came to the big house. 'Maybe I'll get some work here,' he thought, knocking on the door. The housekeeper answered and he asked for work. 'What kind of work can you do?' she asked.

'All kinds of things about the house and I'm a dab hand at looking after cattle and other beasts,' he replied.

'Well, do you think you could take care of hares?'

'I've never done that before but I'm sure I could give it a go. What are the wages?'

'If you take care of the hares all day and bring them all back tonight then you'll get to marry the daughter of the house, but if you don't you'll be hanged.'

Jock was a bit surprised but he thought he would manage, so he agreed.

He was sent down to the field where he too found twenty-four hares and one lame one. The hares were all running around but they stopped and looked at Jock, who swung the pipes up to his mouth and began to play. The hares jumped around to the tune and Jock spent most of the day this way with the hares leaping around and the lame one lying listening to every note. After a while Jock felt a bit hungry so he pulled out the last bit of the bannock and had it for his tea. When it came time to go back he led the hares up the road playing a tune and carrying the lame one inside his jacket. When he got back the master and the housekeeper were delighted to see him and were delighted to hear him play the pipes. It wasn't long before he was married to the daughter of the house and after a time, when the master died, Jock took his place and he lived a long and happy life playing his pipes every day.

A Chick and Her Fellow Travellers

A chick was pecking at a pea-stack when a pea fell on her head and she thought the sky was falling down. She didn't know what to do but thought she would go and tell the King about it because he would know what to do. She walked and walked and walked until she met a hen who asked, 'Where are you going the day, Chick-Lick?'

'I'm going to tell the King the sky is falling down,' she said.

'I'll come with you Chick-Lick,' says the hen.

'Then come along, Hen-Pen,' says the chick.

So they walked and they walked and they walked until they met a cockerel who asked, 'Where are you going the day, Chick-Lick and Hen-Pen?'

'We're going to tell the King the sky is falling down,' they said.

'I'll come with you Chick-Lick and Hen-Pen,' said the cockerel.

'Then come along, Cocky-Lock,' says the chick.

So they walked and they walked and they walked until they met a duck who asked, 'Where are you going the day, Chick-Lick, Hen-Pen and Cocky-Lock?'

'We're going to tell the King the sky is falling down,' said Chick-Lick, Hen-Pen and Cocky-Lock.

'I'll come with you Chick-Lick, Hen-Pen and Cocky-Lock,' said the duck.

'Then come along, Ducky-Daddles,' says the chick.

So they walked and they walked and they walked until they met a goose who asked, 'Where are you going the day, Chick-Lick, Hen-Pen, Cocky-Lock and Ducky-Daddles?'

'We're going to tell the King the sky is falling down,' they said.

'I'll come with you Chick-Lick, Hen-Pen, Cocky-Lock and Ducky-Daddles,' said the goose.

'Then come along, Goosie-Poosie,' says the chick.

So they walked and walked and walked until they met a fox who asked, 'Where are you going the day, Chick-Lick, Hen-Pen, Cocky-Lock, Ducky-Daddles and Goosie-Poosie?'

'We're going to tell the King the sky is falling down,' they say.

And the fox says, 'I'll show you the way, Chick-Lick, Hen-Pen, Cocky-Lock, Ducky-Daddles and Goosie-Poosie.'

So they walked and they walked and they walked until they came to the fox's hole. He shooed them in and he and his young ones ate up Chick-Lick, Hen-Pen, Cocky-Lock, Ducky-Daddles and Goosie-Poosie and they never got to tell the King the sky was falling down.

RASHIECOAT

Rashiecoat was a Princess. Her father, the King, wanted her to get married but she didn't like the man he chose. The King was a stubborn man though and he said she must marry him anyway. But Rashiecoat was just as stubborn so she went to the henwife to ask what she should do.

'Tell your father you won't marry him unless you are given a coat of beaten gold,' said the henwife.

So she went back to her father and told him this. Her father gave her a coat of beaten gold but she still didn't want to marry so she went back to the henwife to ask what she should do.

'Say you won't marry unless you have a coat made of the feathers of all the birds of the air,' said the henwife.

The Princess asked her father and he sent his servants out with bags of oats to call all the birds to take up a grain and leave a feather. Each bird did and the feathers were taken and made into a coat and given to Rashiecoat. But she still didn't want to marry the man after all that.

So she went back to the henwife and asked what she should do.

'Say you won't take him unless you get a coat and slippers made of rushes and that I should make them,' said the henwife.

The King had his servants gather the rushes from the rivers and the henwife wove a coat and slippers and gave it to Rashiecoat. But she still didn't want to marry so she went back to the henwife.

'I can't help you any more,' said the henwife.

So Rashiecoat left her father's house, taking the coats with her. She travelled far and farther and farther still until she came to another King's house where she asked for work. They gave her work in the kitchen.

When Sunday came everyone went to the kirk, but Rashiecoat was left at home to cook the dinner. While she was on her own a little bird came to her and told her to put on the golden coat and go to the kirk.

'I can't do that,' she said, 'I have to cook the dinner.'

The bird said he would cook the dinner and made a spell:

> 'One peat mak another peat burn,
> One spit mak another spit turn,
> One pot mak another pot play,
> Let Rashiecoat gan to the kirk today.'

So she put on the coat and went to the kirk. There the King's son saw her and fell in love with her, but she left before everyone else and he couldn't find out who she was. When she got home she found the dinner cooked and no one knew she'd been out of the house.

The next Sunday, when everyone had gone to the kirk, the bird came again and told her to put on the coat of feathers and go to the kirk and it would cook the dinner. The bird made the spell again:

'One peat mak another peat burn,
One spit mak another spit turn,
One pot mak another pot play,
Let Rashiecoat gan to the kirk today.'

Rashiecoat put on the coat of feathers and went to the kirk. Again she left before everyone else and when the King's son saw her go out he followed her, but she had already disappeared. When she reached home she took off the coat and found the dinner cooked. Nobody knew she had been away.

The next Sunday the bird came back and told her to put on the coat and slippers made of rushes and go to the kirk while the dinner cooked. The bird made the spell again:

'One peat mak another peat burn,
One spit mak another spit turn,
One pot mak another pot play,
Let Rashiecoat gan to the kirk today.'

Rashiecoat put on the coat and slippers and went to the kirk. This time the King's son was sitting near the door. When Rashiecoat slipped out this time he followed her at once but she was still too quick for him and was nowhere to be seen. She ran home but this time she lost one of her slippers. The Prince found it and sent a royal proclamation through all the land that he would marry whoever could put on the slipper. All the ladies of the court and all their ladies-in-waiting tried to put it on but it wouldn't fit any of them. Daughters of merchants and farmers and tradesmen came from far and wide to try on the slipper but it fitted no one. Then a henwife came with her ugly daughter and tried it on. Her mother had nipped and clipped her foot so she could squeeze it on. So the King's son had to say he would marry her. He was riding home with her on his horse when he came to a wood. The little bird who had helped Rashiecoat before was sitting on a branch. When the Prince passed below it sang:

> 'Nippit foot and clippit foot
> Behind the King's son rides,
> But bonnie foot and true foot
> Behind the cauldron hides.'

When the King's son heard this he pushed the henwife's daughter off the horse, took the slipper and rode home. He looked behind the cauldron in the royal kitchen and there he found Rashiecoat. She put the slipper on and it fitted easily. So he married her and they lived happily ever after.

THE BLACK CAT

In Fife there lived a farmer who had a lazy son called Tom who was unwilling to do anything on the farm. Eventually his father told him he would have to find employment somewhere else if he wasn't to help on the farm, so he decided to enlist as a common soldier. He took the bounty but squandered it away on drink and gambling. His commander-in-chief the colonel, who was a harsh man, was not impressed so ordered him abroad.

The governor of the place where he was sent was a cruel man and treated him very badly so Tom deserted from the regiment as soon as he could and fled to a distant part of the country. As he wandered the countryside looking for work he met an old woman and told her his troubles.

She advised him to go to the King and lay his case before His Majesty. He was a fair and good man and would solve all his problems.

So he travelled to the castle but it was night when he got there and too late for an audience with the King, so he was given a room in the tower to sleep in. During the night he was visited by the old woman again. This time she told him that a black cat would come to him before morning and he should talk to it and tell it what he wished for and that he should do what the cat asked of him.

In the middle of the night, as the soldier sat, pensive and uneasy, the cat appeared just as the old woman had predicted.

'Come away my bonny cat,' he said, 'I've been waiting for you for a long time.'

The cat said, 'Who told you to speak?'

He told her about the old woman and the cat said, 'Well, there will be three men come into the room, but don't do anything they ask of you. Ignore them. Wait till someone of higher rank comes and when I brush your leg with my tail, you do as he says.'

In a while three men came into the room and said, 'Rise and let us sit down.' But Tom paid no attention to them.

Another man arrived and said, 'Follow me!' The black cat brushed Tom's leg with its tail so Tom followed the stranger, who spoke to him saying, 'I was King of this castle but was murdered by my factor who then fled abroad and is now your governor. Tell this to my son the King who will see that he is punished and I will never trouble the castle again. The three men you saw here were my murderers and they will do all in their power to stop you.' Then they all vanished.

The soldier went to the King and told him the story he had been told. The King thanked him and gave him a letter, telling him to return to his regiment and deliver it to his commander-in-chief.

Tom travelled as directed and arrived safely back at his regiment. He was recognised by a fellow soldier who, knowing he would be severely punished for his desertion, felt sorry for the young man and tried to hide him. But an officer who also recognised him had him arrested, jailed and afterwards sentenced to death for deserting.

Eventually he was able to persuade one of his jailers to take the King's letter to the commander-in-chief and so was released. The governor was arrested and sent to the King under guard, who commanded him to be executed without judge or jury and Tom was made governor in his place.

Tom made the most of his power. He had the officer who had him arrested reduced to a private and the soldier who had helped him made an officer. He sent for his father and they lived happily ever after.

ROSE RED AND WHITE LILY

Rose Red and White Lily had lost their mother, and their father had remarried. Their stepmother was an evil woman and treated them badly. She had two good sons though, Brown Robin and Arthur, who fell in love with the girls. The young people built a hideaway and there they spent many a day, laughing, playing and making merry. But the stepmother was jealous and vowed to break up their friendship.

She called for her elder son and told him that though it would sadden her, he must go off and make his own way in the world.

'It will sadden me too Mother,' he replied, 'but while I am away, you must treat Rose Red as you would treat me.' She agreed but secretly vowed he would never see his love again.

Then she called for her younger son and told him he too must go off and make his own way in the world, though it would sadden her greatly to see him go.

'It will sadden me too Mother,' he replied, 'but while I am away, you must treat White Lily as you would treat me.' Again she agreed, but secretly vowed they would never meet again.

Brown Robin set off to become a woodsman in the forest and Arthur set off to serve the King at court. But when the girls heard they were going, they planned to leave too and become servants to their lovers. They cut their hair short and dressed as men, taking on men's names. Rose Red became Sweet Willy and White Lily became Roge the Round.

Before the girls went their separate ways, one to the forest and one to the King's Court, they made a vow that if either was in trouble three blasts on a horn would bring one to the other's aid.

Time passed and one day, when Brown Robin and his men were putting the stone, Roge the Round threw it seven feet beyond the rest of them. Having exerted herself so much she had to lean against a tree and in doing so let out a moan that made Brown Robin realise that she was in fact a woman. He took advantage and forty weeks later Roge the Round found herself in need of a midwife. Brown Robin offered his help but she refused, asking him to blow a horn three times as she had a brother at the King's court who would come to her aid at such a sound.

'If you have a brother you love more than me then you can blow the horn yourself,' replied Brown Robin. This she did and

Sweet Willy came at once. But Robin was jealous. No man but him would enter their home without a fight.

Brown Robin and Sweet Willy came to blows and Sweet Willy was wounded. Upset, Sweet Willy decided to declare herself a woman. On hearing this Brown Robin too became upset. 'I wished never to see a woman's blood for the sake of a maid called White Lily,' he declared.

'But she has lived with you for over a year and you didn't know it was she,' declared White Lily.

Meanwhile White Lily gave birth to a son and the word travels round that Brown Robin's man has given birth. The King, when he heard, declared that he must go to the woods himself to investigate this marvel. Arthur asked to accompany the King as he needed to look for a page who had left him. Arriving at the forest Arthur blew his horn and Sweet Willy came running. Arthur asked why he had run away and was told that he needed to see a brother who lived in the forest. The King went in and found Rose Red nursing her son.

Explanations were made and Brown Robin returned from hunting. On finding the King there he was afraid, but the King reassured him, 'Leave this green wood and come to court and be my bowman.'

So the King gave the girls robes of green with girdles of shining gold and Brown Robin and Arthur married Rose Red and White Lily. And as they left the church the girls wondered what their stepmother would say if she could see this sight.

4

ROYAL LEGENDS

THE VISIT OF CHARLES II TO PITTENWEEM

Charles II had been proclaimed King in Edinburgh following the execution of his father and crowned at Scone Palace on New Year's Day 1651. He was accompanied by a lively court for the visit to Fife and the whole district was eager with expectation.

When the news was received by the council in Pittenweem that His Majesty and his court were to travel through the burgh on their way to stay at Anstruther House, they convened a meeting and declared that it was their duty to show their respect by inviting His Majesty to eat and drink as he passed through the town, and so plans were made.

The afternoon before the visit, the town flag was raised on the steeple and the bells began to ring and would remain ringing until he had passed on to Anstruther the next day. The minister, the maillies and the whole council were there in their best clothes. Twenty-four of the ablest men with partizans and another twenty-four with muskets, all dressed in their best clothes too and led by William Sutherland, captain of the guard, awaited His Majesty's arrival at the West Port. When he duly arrived they escorted him and his court through the town until they came to Robert Smith's gate, where a table had been covered with one of his lordship's best carpets and laid with all that His Majesty and his court might wish to eat and drink. There were buns and the best of breads and cakes made with sugar and spice, all prepared by George Hedderwick. There were ten gallons of good strong ale, and bottles of wine and claret all provided by James Richardson and Walter Airth.

The guard attended to the courtiers and the oldest ballie, while the minister attended the King's table and made sure the King knew how grateful and happy the people of Pittenweem were that he had condescended to visit them and how loyal they were to him.

News having reached St Monans that His Majesty had entered Pittenweem, almost the entire population flocked there to see for themselves just what a King looked like. They had very romantic notions of such a powerful person and there was naturally a good deal of excitement at the prospect of seeing the 'Merry Monarch' in the flesh. Even the minister was infected by the occasion and dashed off to the school to persuade his bosom pal the schoolmaster to go with him. The dominie was in full flow when the minister burst into the classroom and called out, 'Behold, the King cometh,' followed by, 'Weel come on then let's go and see him!'

The schoolmaster needed little persuasion and immediately hung up his tawse and gave his pupils a holiday. The two portly gentlemen, huffing and puffing, set off on the Coal Farm Road, leaving their wives, two sisters, to follow and join the crowds in Pittenweem.

As soon as the King showed that he was about to leave and continue his journey to Anstruther a sign was made to Andrew Tod, who was attending the flag on the steeple. He in turn made a signal to the guard who attended the cannon and the whole thirty-six of them were fired at once.

The King having departed, the inhabitants of St Monans trudged back to their work, somewhat disillusioned that the head of their realm was in fact a mere mortal man. One local worthy from St Monans summed up their feelings by declaring, 'Gosh, thae Pittenweem folk mak a din aboot naething. A king is just like ony ither weel-dressed man and if I had lang tails tae my Sabbath-day jacket, I micht be a king masel!'

The Death of Alexander III

It was March 1216 and a gale blasted at Scotland's east coast. Wind-driven, the waves smashed against the cliff base and retreated in angry frustration to gather strength for the next assault. The rider, hurrying ahead of his companions, hugged the now sodden cloak tight to him and wondered again if he should have come. Kicking with spurred heels he encouraged his horse to more speed, and peered at the castle lights he could dimly see glowing ahead. Not far now he promised himself, not far to Kinghorn and the waiting arms of his wife. The horse-man was Alexander III, conqueror of King Haakon of Norway, King of a peaceful prosperous Scotland. Peaceful but still endangered, for the King's first son had not survived childhood and his wife had died in childbirth. That left one other son and when he died at twenty the Scots parliament had no option but to declare the King's granddaughter as heir presumptive.

Any medieval kingdom with an infant monarch was open to interference from her neighbours, especially if the child was female, so Alexander hurriedly remarried. He was only forty-five, time yet to make a male heir to ensure the stability of the realm.

Six months after his marriage to Yolande of Dreux, Alexander had to leave her in Kinghorn while he travelled to Edinburgh across the Forth. Business concluded the King was about to set off for Yolande when he was warned to stay put. None other than Thomas the Rhymer predicted, 'Alas for tomorrow, a day of calamity and misery. Before the twelfth hour shall be the sorest wind and tempest that ever was heard of in Scotland.'

Perhaps Alexander hesitated. Thomas the Rhymer had a powerful reputation but the King's wife had an even more powerful allure – they were newlyweds after all – and the King decided to make the journey. Outside the wind was already rising and its shrieking in the battlements of Edinburgh Castle might have reminded the King of another occasion.

The day of his wedding at Jedburgh Abbey, the town filled with noblemen from Scotland and France, rich silks and velvet, high-bred laughter and nuptial anticipation. There were pipes and harps and lutes, swordsmen displaying their skills, tables piled with food all lit by flickering torches, then a masked man entered the company. A mummer some said, but none were sure who as the man paraded through the crowd dressed as a skeleton and dancing to the music. He came to the King where he sat with his new Queen and pointed a bony finger at the couple. Yolande shuddered and hid her face behind cupped hands, the bishop advanced, cross upraised, and the skeleton vanished as dramatically as it had appeared. The whole episode left a chill.

Some claimed the skeleton had been a one-time lover of Yolande, a soldier who shortly after entered Melrose Abbey and laughed at mention of the masque.

Some years before, Michael Scot, the wizard of Balwearie, had met his King on the cliffs above Kinghorn and prophesied that his favourite horse would cause the death of the monarch. It is told that, shaken by a sudden gust of rage inherited from his Celtic ancestors, Alexander stabbed the unfortunate animal on the spot and rode away on another charger.

Alexander, however, was also a warrior and no man to be frightened of portents or weird warnings. He took a small escort with him as he rode for the ferry. The ferryman was not keen to chance the choppy water but hid his fear behind his words: 'I could not die better than in the company of your father's son.'

They landed safely at Inverkeithing where the master of the salt works, obviously an old friend, advised the King to stay the night. 'How many times have I tried to persuade you that midnight travelling will bring you no good?'

Alexander did not make it to his wife. At a stretch of clifftop coastline, only a short distance from the castle, in a sudden gleam of misty moonlight the white bones of the horse he had slain lay before him on the top of the cliff. His steed took fright, shied and threw the startled King, who fell from the edge of the crag. His body was found the next morning, his neck broken, by a poor Fifer, Murdoch Shanks. Of all Scotland he was the only man to profit from the death of the King as he was granted lands for his discovery.

The course of history was changed. There is a Celtic cross to mark the spot where Alexander III fell. A reminder of what might have been.

THE GUDEMAN OF BALLENGEIGH

Both King James IV and V had many strange and ludicrous adventures in the guise of the Gudeman of Ballengeigh which are said to have taken place in the neighbourhood of Falkland Palace, where they often stayed. These adventures formed many a tale told round the fires in the hearths of cottages in Fife.

The King and the Gypsies

According to one such tale James IV was one day wandering incognito about the country when he fell in with a band of Gypsies and went with them to where they had set up in the Weymss Cave, now known as the Court Cave. After much merrymaking and drinking a fight broke out amongst the Gypsies. James tried to make the peace but they would have none of it. Eventually he threw off his homespun disguise and revealed his true identity. Immediately the fighting stopped and the gang drank his health and escorted him on his way.

The King and the Robbers

Another time he was traversing the old road from Cupar by Kennoway to Kinghorn and had reached Clatto, or more properly 'Clettie Den', a furlong from the castle of the same name, the stronghold of the fierce Setons who were accustomed to hold up travellers. There, the apparently unarmed wayfarer was set upon by a youth who seized his bridle. To the surprise of the assailant the traveller drew a concealed weapon and in an instant severed the hand that grasped the reins. The bandit fled. Picking up the bleeding hand, James rode on. Next day he appeared in state at Clatto Castle and asked an interview with the laird and his sons. One, he was told, was confined to bed, the result of an accident. The anxious monarch desired to see him and feel his pulse. It was the left hand that was withdrawn from under the covers. The King asked to feel the other. When at last the youth admitted he had lost it James produced the hand from his pocket and asked if it would fit him. The Setons had long been a terror to the countryside, making use of a subterranean passage from their castle to the Den where it ended in a cave from which they pounced on unsuspecting travellers. James had an unrelenting sense of justice and forthwith did away with the whole family.

The taste for adventure was hereditary and it is of his son, James V, that the following tales are told.

The King and the Miller

On one of his excursions James V is said to have gone into the miller's house in a place called Ballomill on the north bank of the Eden. It was evening and he asked for lodgings for the night. The evening passed very agreeably and the miller was delighted with the conversation and company of his lodger. So much so, in fact, that he called for his wife to bring 'the hen that sat next to the cock and make her ready for supper.' When they sat down to supper, the miller was all for the stranger taking the head of the table. The King pretended to be shy about doing this because he was a stranger but this only made the miller add, 'Sit up, for I will have strangers honoured.' The King was obliged to comply.

The next morning the King had the miller accompany him as far as the place where his courtiers were appointed to meet him. When the miller saw the courtiers he was a little astonished and a bit embarrassed at finding himself in the presence of His Majesty and finding that he had entertained him as his guest. The King, however, because he enjoyed the hospitality of the miller, insisted he accompany him to Falkland Palace, where he could return the favour. The miller, this time, was obliged to comply.

Later, about to sit down to supper at Falkland, the King insisted the miller took the head of the table. The miller tried to decline but the King, giving him a slap on the head and using the miller's own words, said, 'Sit up, for I will have strangers honoured.'

Well, the miller ended up staying about ten days at the palace, and being a strong athletic man took part in many games and sports against the courtiers such as tossing the bar and putting the stone, beating them often as not. However, it was observed that, despite the fine feeding at the King's table, the miller gradually became weaker. In fact, the longer he stayed the weaker he became. This made His Majesty ask him what he usually fed on to which he replied, 'broken water and slain meal'. The fine food was obviously doing him no good

When he was about to leave for home the King asked him whether he would choose the eighth part or the second part of Ballomill. The miller, it seems, was not a very good accountant and thinking the eighth part sounded best, he chose it. Accordingly he got an eighth part of the land instead of a half. It was made over to him in a Crown Charter with the liberty to hunt all the way to the gates of Melville House, something which he and his heirs enjoyed for many a year and all because he had given the King a night's lodging.

The King and the Minister

On another occasion King James V fell in with a minister of Markinch. The King thought him rather dim-witted so he left four questions for his consideration. The minister was to deliver the answers at an appointed time and place but it was intimated that if he did not answer them satisfactorily the minister would be put out of office and lose his allowance.

The first question was: 'Where is the middle of the earth?'

The second was: 'How long would I take to go round the world?'

The third was: 'How much am I worth?'

And the fourth was: 'What am I thinking?'

All hard questions for the poor minister, who didn't know the answer to any of them.

Now a little south of Markinch, on the bank of the River Leven, below the Plasterers Inn, there was a mill called the Middle Mill. The miller was said to be a witty, ingenious sort of man and was said to look very like the minister of Markinch. The miller, hearing about the minister's difficulties over the questions, went to see the minister and offered to meet the King in his place and try to answer the questions for him in return for a suit of his best clothes. Much relieved, the poor minister cheerfully agreed. It was also agreed that, if the miller answered the questions to the King's satisfaction, he should also intercede on behalf of the minister so that he could continue in his living. Accordingly, when the time arrived, the miller was waiting for the King at the appointed place.

'Where is the middle of the earth?' the King asked. The miller put out his stick and said, 'It is just there,' adding that if His Majesty cared to measure all around he would find that it was just where the point of his stick was. The King thought he'd rather take his word for it rather than measure for himself so he asked the second question.

'How long would it take me to go round the world?'

'Well, if you get up with the sun and follow it around all day then it will take you exactly twenty-four hours.' The King was well pleased with that answer and thought it just as ingenious as the first. So he asked the third question.

'How much am I worth?'

The answer given was that he should be worth about twenty-nine pieces of silver because Our Lord was only valued at thirty pieces of silver and the King should certainly be valued at a penny less than Our Lord was valued. The King was equally pleased with that answer.

'Now,' he said, 'you have answered so well that perhaps you could tell me what I am thinking?'

The answer was, 'You are thinking that I am the minister of Markinch but in fact I am the miller of the Middle Mill.'

'Well,' said the King, 'you shall have his job and he shall be turned out.'

'If it pleases Your Majesty,' replied the miller, 'we have already made an agreement as to that. I was to intercede for him to Your Majesty that he should remain in his job.' And we believe that the King agreed.

The King and the Dominie

Then there is the story of the drinking bout in the change house in Markinch. The King in his guise of a gudeman asked for refreshment but the landlady informed him that the only room she had was already occupied with the minister and the schoolmaster. It seemed though that they had no objection to admitting the stranger to their company. He was made very welcome and began to drink with them. After several hours of drinking, during which the King succeeded in completely ingratiating himself with the two local dignitaries, it was time to pay the bill and James pulled out money to pay his share. The schoolmaster suggested to the minister that they should pay it all as the stranger had only recently joined them and he was as a stranger entitled to their hospitality. The schoolmaster would have let him off easily but the minister thought otherwise.

'Na, na! I see nae reason in that. The birkie maun pay eeksie-peeksie wi oorsels. That's aye the law in Markinch. Eeksie-peeksie's the word.'

The schoolmaster tried to change this selfish and unjust reasoning but the minister remained stubborn.

King James at last cried out in a fit of temper, 'Weel, weel, eeksie-peeksie be it!' He immediately made such arrangements as ensured the wages of both his drinking companions were equal. And so through the centuries, until school boards and the like came to upset the order of things, the salaries of the minister and the schoolmaster in Markinch were as equal as they could be.

The King and the Shepherd

It was on the banks of the Rossie Loch in the heart of the marshes and woods of Lathrisk, about one and a half miles north of Falkland, that King James had an encounter with a shepherd mending his shoes. He entered into conversation with the shepherd and amongst other things asked him, 'Wha stays in that muckle hoose there?' pointing to the palace towering over the thatched cottages.

'It's some man they ca' the King, but we just ca' him Jamie the Gudeman,' said the shepherd.

'Aye, and what sort o' man is he, that gudeman?' asked the King.

'I didnae ken muckle about him but they say he makes a deal o' dirty knights.'

Meantime the sheep went astray and the shepherd had to go and turn them, leaving his shoe and awl behind. In his absence the King took the awl and put it in his pocket. When the shepherd returned he found his shoe but no awl. He looked about, searching for it, saying, 'I wonder where it is? I'm sure I left it here.'

The King replied, 'That's as much saying, sir, that I stole it.' But the shepherd said, 'I'm not saying you stole it but I'm sure I left it here and if somebody had left it be it would still be here.'

'That's still saying that I have stolen it,' said the King.

'I'm no saying you stole it but I left it here and it wouldn't have gone home on its own,' replied the shepherd.

'That's still saying the same, sir, that I stole it,' replied the King once more.

In the meantime, the nobles arrived to fetch the King and the poor shepherd learned who he had been talking to so freely and half accusing of stealing his awl. The King rewarded him in his own humorous way. He made him strip naked and wade up to the neck in the mire and moss of Rossie Loch. Then when he came out, mud-covered from head to toe, he drew his sword and knighted him.

'Mony a dirty knight I've made but sic a dirty ane as you never till this day.' And then he gave him the lands of Lathrisk to live on.

THE MAGGIE LAUDER STORY

Maggie Lauder has long since been known as a bit of an Anstruther character with many stories attributed to her and a popular song written about her. Some say she was the wife of William de Anstruther who occupied the Castle o' Dreel, others say she was the sister of Sir Robert Lauder and places her in a snug wee house on the East Green. Whoever she was, there were three things she was celebrated for. She had a lightness of foot which made her a bonnie dancer. She had a strong heart which gave her the courage to stand up to plundering soldiers, as well as having the strength to carry a grown man on her back. She was also known to be fond of roaming the countryside.

One time King James himself, travelling in the guise of a piper on one of his journeys about Fife, came to the ford on the Dreel Burn, which at that time didn't have a bridge. The burn was in spate and he found he couldn't cross it without getting his feet wet. He was standing there wondering what to do when a woman marched up. The King explained that he didn't want to get wet and without any hesitation the woman, Maggie Lauder herself, caught him up and carried him on her back to the other side. James was impressed, so when he reached the other bank with his feet still dry, he concluded the meeting by handing her his purse. What we don't know, however, is whether the identity of the generous traveller was ever revealed. I like to think it was.

Another time, as she travelled one day on the highways and byways of Fife, Maggie met up with another traveller, a wandering piper who had the cheek to ask her what her name was, only to be told, 'Get awa wi ye, you hallanshaker, get on yer wey, you bladderskate.' Then she relented and replied, 'My name is Maggie Lauder.'

But the piper wasn't to be put off. 'It's braw tae meet sic a bonny lassie,' he said. 'Come and sit doon beside me. I'll no herm ye, I'm a piper tae trade and when the lassies hear me blaw up ma chanter they just cannae stop themselves dancing. Ye've mebee heard o' me. My name is Rob the Ranter.'

'Weel if you're Rob then I've heard o' ye,' said Maggie. 'A' the lassies frae near and far have heard o' Rob the Ranter. Hae ye yer bags wi' ye? Is yir drone in order? Then blaw up yir chanter and I'll shake ma fit richt weel.'

Well, Rob didn't need to be told twice. He picked up his pipes and started to play such a braw tune that Maggie jumped up and began to dance.

On and on she danced and on and on he played until they both collapsed, exhausted.

'Weel, ye fairly played yir pairt,' said Maggie. 'Yir face is like the crimson. I've no heard onybody play like that in the hale o' Scotland.'

'Weel it's worth ma while when I hae sic a dancer as you,' replied Rob.

'Weel, I live up Anster wey and if ye ever come tae Anster Fair, be sure tae spier fir Maggie Lauder.' Whether he did or not, the story doesn't tell us.

Another story tells us of her courage. Her brother, Sir Robert, had a farm where he stored his corn in sacks in the granary. A troop of soldiers were encamped nearby and their captain sent a party of them to seize the corn for their own use. Sir Robert was away at the time but his sister, Mistress Margaret, was there. Sir Robert's servants being too few in number to resist came to tell her. The story goes that Maggie at once called for a sharp knife and a strong flail. Having got these she entered the granary and after giving the raiders a right tongue-lashing for their law-lessness, she slashed the sacks with the knife and scattered the corn. And then she began to birl the flail around her so enthusi-astically that the soldiers took flight and left her to it.

THE KING'S BOX

I first heard this story from Duncan Williamson, a Scottish traveller originally from the west coast but who settled in Fife in his later years. I've heard the story told by other storytellers and placed in other parts of the country but this is how I remember Duncan telling it to me.

King Malcom really liked being King. Why wouldn't he? He had a big house in Dunfermline to live in, servants to do all the work and soldiers to fight his battles. But what he liked best about being King was that he got lots of presents. Folk came from all over to visit him and they always brought him a present. He just loved presents.

Living not far from Dunfermline was an old farmer who had long wanted to meet the King in person. Many a day he spent in a little hut in the woods until he had made something he thought the King would accept as a present.

One day he travelled to the town and knocked on the door of the palace. When the King's servant answered the old man demanded, 'I want to see the King.'

'No, no, the King doesn't speak to the likes of you,' answered the servant. 'Away you go round the back to the kitchen and see the cook. She'll give you something to eat and drink.'

'But I've brought him a present,' said the old man.

Now the servant knew how much the King liked getting presents and he didn't want to get on his wrong side so he answered, 'Wait there a minute, I'll go and ask.'

So he went to find the King and said, 'There's an old man at the door wanting to see you. He says he has a present for you.'

'A present?' said the King. 'Show him in then.'

So the old man was shown into the King's chamber and he handed him a box.

'Thank you,' said the King. 'Now away you go to the kitchen and get something to eat and drink.'

The King looked at the box and saw it was beautifully carved and when he opened it he read, 'Gie it tae the wan you love.'

'Well,' he thought, 'who do I love? There's my faithful deerhound. He's served me well for many a year. I could give it to him but he'd just chew it. No, I suppose I'd better give it to the wife.'

So he went to the Queen's chambers and called, 'Wife, I have a present for you.' Now the Queen wasn't used to getting presents so she was surprised. 'Thank you, Your Majesty,' she said, taking the box. She saw the bonny carving and found the writing inside. 'Gie it tae the wan you love.'

'Now,' she thought, 'who can I give it to? There's the captain of the guard. He's been looking very sad since his wife died. I'll give it to him.'

So she went down to the stables and found the captain of the guard. 'Sir, I have a present for you,' she said, handing him the box.

The captain thanked her and slipped it into his jacket and carried on seeing to his horse. Later when he was back in his rooms he took out the box and looked at it. He too saw the bonny carving and found the writing when he opened it. 'Gie it tae the wan you love,' he read. 'Sadly the one I love has passed away, but I could give it to my son.'

So he went to his son's rooms and, handing him the box, said, 'Son, I have a present for you.' His son took it and he too noticed the bonny carving and when he opened it read, 'Gie it tae the wan you love.'

'Now, who could I give it to? Well, I've had my eye on wee Jeannie, the kitchen maid, for a while. Maybe if I give her a present my luck will be in.' So he went down into the kitchen and found Jeannie. 'I've got a present for you,' he said and handed her the box. Now, nobody had ever given her a present before, so she blushed and curtsied as she thanked the young lad, and slipped it into her apron pocket before going back to her work. Later when she was back in her room she took it out and looked at it. She too saw the bonny carving and found the writing inside. 'Gie it tae the wan you love.' Now, who do I love? she thought. Well there is someone who has put a roof over my head, put food in my belly. Yes, I'll give it to the King.

Next morning she made her way to the King's chambers and found the King. 'Your Majesty, I have a present for you.' She handed him the box. The King took it and smiled. 'Thank you, lass,' he said. When she had gone he looked again at the box and thought, 'I should have just given it to the dog in the first place.'

THE LEGEND OF QUEEN MARGARET

Queen Margaret of Scotland, also known as Margaret of Wessex, was an English Princess of the House of Wessex. Margaret was sometimes called 'The Pearl of Scotland'.

Born in exile in Hungary, Margaret and her family returned to England in 1057, but fled to the Kingdom of Scotland following the Norman conquest of England in 1066. Around 1070 Margaret married Malcolm III of Scotland, becoming Scottish Queen. Legend has it that when she arrived in Scotland and was walking to Dunfermline from the landing place on the Forth, she complained of being tired. Coming upon a huge Saxon stone about two miles from the King's residence, she sat down on it to rest and on her subsequent journeys to and fro, she often used it as a resting place. It became known as St Margaret's Stone and the nearby farm became known as St Margaret's Stone Farm.

She was known to be a pious woman, and among many charitable works she established a ferry across the Firth of Forth for pilgrims travelling to Dunfermline Abbey, which gave the towns of South Queensferry and North Queensferry their names.

She is credited with having a civilizing influence on her husband Malcolm by reading him stories from the Bible. She instigated religious reform, trying hard to make the worship and practices of the Church in Scotland conform with those of Rome. She also worked to bring the Scottish Church practice in line with that of the continental church of her childhood. Due to these achievements, she was considered an example of the 'just ruler', and influenced her husband and children – especially her youngest son, later David I – also to be just and righteous rulers.

In her private life, Margaret was as devout as she was in her public duties. She spent much of her time in prayer, devotional reading, and ecclesiastical embroidery. This appears to have had a considerable effect on the more uncouth Malcolm, who could not read; he so admired her devotion that he had her books decorated in gold and silver.

Situated a short distance from Tower Hill in Dunfermline and from the mound on which the town stands is a cave named after her. The legend regarding this place is that Queen Margaret was known to frequently retire to this secluded spot to pray in private. Her husband, not knowing what she went there for or doubting that this was her true purpose, secretly followed her. He looked into the cave to see what she was up to, believing she was in fact conducting an affair, as was common at that time amongst the nobility. Seeing her engaged in devotions he was quite overjoyed, and, possibly because he felt guilty, ordered the cave to be suitably fitted out for her use.

Malcolm seems to have been largely ignorant of the long-term effects of Margaret's endeavours, not being especially religious himself. He was content for her to pursue her reforms as she wished, a testament to the strength and affection inherent in their marriage.

Queen Margaret was canonised in 1250 by Pope Innocent IV in recognition of her personal holiness, fidelity to the Church, work for religious reform, and charity.

Another old legend informs us that on the eve of the Battle of Largs in 1263 it was believed by the Scots that the Royal Tombs at Dunfermline gave up their dead and that there passed through the northern porch to war against the mighty Norway a lofty and blooming matron in royal attire, leading in her right hand a noble knight resplendent in arms and a crown on his head, and followed by three heroic warriors similarly armed and crowned; these were Margaret and her husband Malcom and their three sons, founders of the medieval Church of Scotland.

5

SAINTS, SINNERS
AND ROGUES

THE LEGEND OF ST SERF

According to the legend, Serf was the second son of Eliud, King of Canaan, and his wife Alphia, daughter of a King of Arabia. As a young man Serf went to Rome, where his sanctity was so obvious that he was elected Pope, a post he filled for seven years. He then travelled across Europe, eventually finding himself in what is now Scotland. Here he established a religious community, on St Serf's Inch, an island on Loch Leven. From here he seems to have moved to Dunning in Perthshire, establishing a church there (and, according to legend, slaying a dragon that was terrorising the residents) before moving south and settling at Culross in Fife.

At the time, Adamnan was Abbot of Scotland and on hearing of Serf's arrival, he rushed to meet him on the island of Inchkeith in the Firth of Forth, where he greeted Serf with great admiration having heard such good things about him. Their time together there was spent in great discussion and debate, which pleased them both. Eventually Serf asked of Adamnan, 'How shall I dispose of my household and companions?' Meaning, where should they settle.

Adamnan replied, 'Let them dwell in the land of Fife, from the sea of the Britains and to the mountains they call Ochil.' And so it was done.

He settled in Culross, where he cleared all the thorns and thistles which grew there in great abundance.

But the King of Scots, namely, Bruce, son of Dagart who then ruled the Kingdom of the Picts, flew into a rage because Serf hadn't asked his permission to settle in Fife. The King sent soldiers to kill Serf and his entire household. But a violent disease came over the King and he nearly died. Hastily he changed his plans, sending for Serf and asking that he should restore his health in return for the gift of being allowed to live in the place which he and his companions had chosen. Serf was moved by the King's pleas and restored his health, so was allowed to settle in Culross.

While living in Fife, Serf and some of his monks sometimes took themselves off to a cave at Dysart for prayer and reflection. On one occasion one of his monks took ill and desperately wanted a drink of wine. There wasn't any, but St Serf took the water from the fountain which was there, blessed it and changed it into wine and the sick man was healed. Again in that cave when St Serf was lying on his bed, the Devil came to him, tempting him and arguing with him. 'Are you the wise cleric, Serf?' he asked.

'What do you want, miserable creature?' asked Serf.

'I wish to debate with you and question you a little,' replied the Devil.

'Begin, miserable wretch, begin!' answered Serf.

They entered into much discussion but Serf was able to counter all the Devil's arguments and questions. In the end the Devil admitted that Serf had won.

'You are wise, Serf, and I can argue with you no more.'

'Go then, you wretched creature,' said St Serf, 'go and quickly leave this place, and never again try to come back and appear here to any man.' In honour of St Serf the cave at Dysart was deemed sacred for many a year.

According to another legend, a coracle came ashore at Culross. Its only passenger was Princess Theneva (later St Theneva), who was heavily pregnant at the time. Her father, King Loth of the Gododdin, who ruled from Traprain Law, responded to her pregnancy by first trying to kill her, then casting her adrift in a coracle. On arrival at Culross, Princess Theneva gave birth to a boy. Serf is also said to have been closely linked with St Kentigern having taken him and his mother in when he was a baby, overseeing his education and giving him the pet-name Mungo.

When he had first arrived at Culross, Serf had thrown away a branch he had brought with him from across the sea and where it landed, an apple tree grew. Then in a vision he was told that this was where his body should be buried. St Serf is said to have been buried under this tree on the 1st of July, a date on which he is celebrated still in Culross.

The Legend of St Kentigern (St Mungo)

At the east end of Culross on the sea coast lies the remains of a chapel known as St Mungo's Chapel. Legend has it that this is on or near the spot where Kentigern, later to be given the name Mungo by his benefactor Serf, was born. Kentigern's mother was Thanetis, daughter of Lothus, King of the Picts. She is said to have become pregnant after being raped. Her furious father on hearing of her condition tried to kill her by throwing her from the heights of Trapain Law but she survived. Some say her father then cast her adrift in a coracle, others that she ran away, stealing a boat which drifted across the River Forth to be cast up on the coast where Culross now is. Thanetis was found by shepherds just after giving birth, the child wrapped in rags and lying in the open air.

At that time Serf was living in the same place, teaching the sacred literature to many boys. The shepherds took the young woman and her child to Serf, who baptised them, calling the mother Taneu and the child Kyntyern. When he reached a suitable age the child began his education. The fellow pupils of Kentigern were jealous of him because he was an obvious favourite and they were always plotting against him in many ways.

One day when Serf was away the boys began to play with a little bird, which on account of the colour of its breast was called a redbreast. This bird was accustomed to being fed by Serf himself and was quite tame. The boys snatched it from each other so roughly that its head was torn from its body. The boys plotted amongst themselves to blame Kentigern. When he heard this the boy took the bird in his hand, put the head on the body and made the sign of the cross. Straightaway the bird revived and rose into the air to meet Serf as it usually did.

It was a rule of Serf that each boy whom he taught should take turns to look after the lamps in the church by day and by night and while the others slept should attend to the fire to ensure there was always light in the church. One time Kentigern was taking his turn and attending to his duties diligently when his rivals secretly put out all the fires within the monastery. Then as if ignorant and innocent they went to bed. When Kentigern arose at dawn to attend to the lights he looked for fire everywhere but could find none. At length when he realised what his rivals had done he went back to the house and cut down a branch of a hazel tree, signed it with the sign of the cross and breathed on it. A wonderful and remarkable thing followed. Straightaway flames shot from the sky, setting the branch alight and lighting up the darkness. So he was able to light all the church lamps in time for the service. All the other pupils were astonished when they saw the branch burn without being consumed. In the end the fire went out when all the lamps were lit. The hazel tree from which the branch was taken was blessed by Kentigern and afterwards grew into a wood. To this day the locals say that even the greenest branch taken from this wood catches fire instantly, as if it was the driest of wood.

Serf had a cook, someone who was excellent at his job and as such was extremely important to Serf and those who stayed with him. The cook took ill and eventually died. Everyone knew it would not be easy to replace him. On the day after his burial Serf was approached by servants, family and followers. They pleaded with him to send for Kentigern and compel him to try to raise the cook from the dead. They persisted, trying to persuade Serf to comply. The old man hesitated at first, reluctant to ask the young man to do such a thing, but eventually he decided he should ask him to at least try. The young man went to the tomb where the cook had been buried the day before and removed the earth with which he was covered. He fell on the ground with a tearstained face and prayed. While Kentigern prayed, the body lying in the dust rose up and left the tomb and, at Kentigern's command, once more resumed his duties in the kitchen, living for another seven years.

Kentigern, however, realised that this incident would make him even more of a target amongst his fellow pupils. Deciding he could no longer live amongst those who had such malice against him, he secretly left Fife.

THE LEGEND OF ST ANDREW AND ST RULE

Many miles separate the beach at Capernaum from the sands of eastern Fife but they are united forever by the name of a saint. Andrew, according to the Bible, was a fisherman on the Sea of Galilee; he met Jesus, abandoned the search for fish and became one of the original twelve disciples. He trod the dusty roads of the eastern Roman Empire for three decades before being martyred at Patras in Greece.

The Scottish connection begins seven centuries later when a ship from Patras was driven by a storm onto the shores of Fife and one of the survivors, Rule or Regulus, landed there. Legend states that in AD 345 Regulus, a Greek monk born in Achaia, and an abbot in the town of Patros, was told by an angel in a visionary dream that the Emperor Constantine had decided to remove St Andrew's relics from Patras to Constantinople, and in some retellings, that Constantine was about to invade Patras. For safekeeping, Regulus was to move as many relics as he could as far away as possible, to the western ends of the earth, where he should found a church dedicated to St Andrew.

These relics were bones: a kneecap, an arm bone, one tooth and three fingers of a long-dead man, but such things were venerated throughout the Dark and Middle Ages. He carried the relics through the seas of the Mediterranean to Portugal and with great trouble he travelled over the northern seas before being shipwrecked on the coast of Fife at a settlement once known as Muckross and later Kilrymont or Kilrule but now known as St Andrews.

Nothing was saved except a few of the men who came with the relics and the bones themselves. When the news got round the country, the King of the Picts, Óengus, and his people came from all over with rich offerings to wonder at the relics of the holy Apostle. It is said that the King of the Picts and his people were saved by St Rule and his fellow monks and converted by songs and prayers and other divine ceremonies. Then Óengus, overcome by religious fervour, fell on his knees and with much reverence kissed the blessed relics. He built a kirk there, dedicated in honour of St Andrew and decorated with cups and chalices and other sundry rich jewels of gold and silver to remain there for ever in the honour of the saint. The descendants of Óengus and the Scots when the Picts were exiled from the realm have since held St Andrew in highest reverence as patron saint of Scotland.

The Legend of St Fillan

Some legends tell us that St Fillan was born in Fife in the seventh century. His father Feriath was a nobleman and his mother was Kentigerna. At birth he was said to have had the appearance of a monster and had a stone in his mouth. His father was so horrified by his appearance that he secretly ordered his servant to drown the boy in a nearby loch. He was thrown in but he didn't die. They say he was looked after under the water by 'angels' before being found accidentally by a bishop called Ibarus, who rescued the child and had him baptised. The bishop brought him up in the monastery of Pittenweem, educating him to a high standard. Later, when the bishop died, Fillan was chosen to be bishop in his place.

While he was in the monastery he secretly built a cell away from the cloister so he could study and contemplate in private. One night a young servant was sent to tell him that supper was ready. The servant being curious as to what was going on, knelt and peered through a chink in the door. He saw Fillan writing in the dark with a clear light shining from his left hand lighting up his right hand enough for him to see. The servant, much

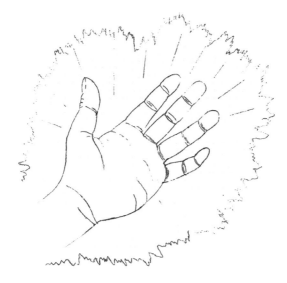

amazed by what he had seen, hurried back to tell his story to the other brothers. When Fillan found out that his secret had been revealed he was angry with the servant. A domesticated crane who lived in the monastery took it upon itself to punish the servant by pecking out his eyes and blinding him. But Fillan was moved by compassion when he heard and straightaway restored his eyes.

THE BLACK POCKETBOOK

Thomas Adamson, a well-to-do Fife farmer, having been very successful one market day at Dunfermline was able to stuff his black pocketbook with banknotes. He was in great humour as you might imagine and after having a good blether and a dram or two with some of his farmer friends and acquaintances, was preparing to leave the market when he was approached by a tall, dark-complexioned man in the dress of a drover.

'Hoo's a' wi' ye the day, Master Adamson?' he asked. 'Man I'm glad tae see ye, I've been seeking for ye owre the hail market.'

'Weel friend,' said Tam, 'what dae ye want wi' me noo that ye have fund me?'

'Is your cattle a' selt?' asked the stranger.

'Every wan o' them. I hae made a great market the day,' replied Tam.

'So it seems. I'll need tae look elsewhere.' So saying, the stranger walked quickly away.

'I don't like the look of him,' thought Tam to himself as he slowly left the market. 'I never saw him before and he doesn't seem to be a drover either.'

'I hope all is right,' he thought as his hand and his thoughts returned to the pocketbook. But it was gone. Tam stood as if he had been turned to stone. At length he began to exclaim, 'I'm lost, ruined, and I'll need to flee the country. How can I ever look my wife and bairns in the eye without my pocketbook? The devil catch that villain. If I had him here I'd teach him to steal an honest man's pocketbook. A good hundred and fifty pounds sterling and seventeen and six in silver was in there. What am I to do?'

A question much easier asked than answered. And he wasn't in the right mind to answer it at that moment. All he could do was moan.

Eventually he began to come back to his senses. 'I'll go back to the market and fetch out the constables and the militia and the fire drum. All the town will hear of it.' And having decided on a course of action, he returned to the market.

In the meantime, Tam's wife was on her way to Dunfermline to make a few purchases at the same market. She hadn't been ready to leave in the morning with her husband. She had arrived within a half mile of the town when she heard a sweet voice singing as if to a child, and on approaching nearer she could hear the words:

'Sleep baby sleep!
Though thy fond mother's breast
Where thy young head reclines
Is a stranger to rest?'

Almost at the same moment she saw a young woman in a red
cloak sitting alone in a lonely part of the road, nursing a child.
As she drew nearer she saw that the young woman's eyes were
red with crying. Mrs Adamson's sympathies were aroused so she
stopped and asked, 'What the matter wi' ye lass?'

'My husband, my husband, he has gone to market and I hope
and pray he will not have occasion to stick to his bargain.'

'Is that all? My man has gone to the market tae and he'll
make many a bargain but I'll no be greetin' about them.'

'Oh but I'm no like you and my situation is no like yours,'
said the young woman as she burst into tears. And so did Mrs
Adamson.

Then suddenly the lassie sat up and looked over in the direction of Dunfermline. 'Did you hear that? There again, shouts
and uproar. They will murder him! It's over! If you knew what
I have had to endure today you would pity me. I've sat here on
this cold stone from morning till now with no one to smile at
me, no one to comfort me but my baby. I have sat here watching the birds and wishing I had wings like them to fly away but
where would I fly to, but to him who, however cold to others,
warms to me and his baby. And could I forsake him when all,
even his own family, have gone against him? No!'

She paused and Mrs Adamson began to think the woman
was deranged.

The young woman continued, 'I can't endure the torture of
not knowing any longer. If he won't come to me I will go to him!'

She paused. 'Good woman, might I ask you a favour?'

'Aye, anything in my power,' said Mrs Adamson.

'Take charge of my baby till my return. I am going down to the market to look for my husband. I won't be long.'

'Willingly, if you'll not be too long. I've business myself in the town and need to look for my own husband, who no doubt will be in the public house with some of his cronies.'

The young woman hastily kissed the bairn and handed it over, taking off her red cloak and throwing it round the shoulders of Mrs Adamson. 'You might get cold waiting and I won't need it.'

The bairn, finding itself in strange arms, soon began to yell, so Mrs Adamson began to sing it to sleep. Just as she had succeeded and was making it a comfortable bed on her lap, a tall dark man strode past, threw a black pocketbook into her lap and quickly disappeared.

'What's this?' she cried, too astonished to pay attention to where the man went. Then she exclaimed, 'It's my Tam's pocketbook. And it's full of notes. Am I seeing things? Am I bewitched? Or is the pocketbook bewitched? There's something no right in the wind. I wish that lassie was back for her bairn. I hope she doesn't mean to leave it with me altogether. I wonder what Tam would think if I brought hame a bairn that wisnae mine. I don't understand at all except that Tam has lost his pocketbook and I have found it.'

But whatever her suspicions about the lassie were, they disappeared when she returned. 'Did you find your husband?'

'No, I didn't see anything of him and could get no word of him.'

'Weel, weel, here's your bairn and your cloak. Take my advice and gan hame. He's no worth fretting ower.'

Mrs Adamson hurried to the market and found her husband in a state of distraction, asking everybody if they had seen his pocketbook. As soon as he saw his wife he poured out the whole sorry story. 'I canna hold my heid up after this. I might as well die at the back of the dyke!'

'It's no as bad as that Tam. Come away from the market and I'll tell you something that'll maybe astonish you.'

'Awa wi' ye woman, it's no time for jokes and stories.'

'Tam, I've found it. Here it is! Here's your pocketbook!'

'So it is. The very same. Where did you get it? Let me see if it's all safe? Aye it's a' there. I think you deserve a new gown for your luck. I'll treat ye.'

Ever after the story of the black pocketbook formed one of his most amusing stories when Tam had around him a circle of friends at his cosy fireside on a winter's night.

DUNCAN SCHULEBRED'S VISION

Duncan Shulebred was a handloom weaver in Dunfermline. He wasn't well liked because he was seen to be hard in his dealings with customers and even dishonest. He was also very fond of a dram and took every opportunity to get drunk, always at someone else's expense. He would meet with a crony or two of an evening in some public house, drink with them, then before it was time to settle the bill he would quietly slip out on some pretext or other, saying he would be back but not coming back, thus leaving the others to pay the publican, a trick commonly known locally as 'singing the cobbler'. Duncan, like many other weavers, worked his loom over one half of the year and spent the other half hawking his cloth around Dunfermline and as far as Edinburgh.

One time he sold some of his cloth to a small-time Edinburgh lawyer, Andrew Gavin. After being paid he invited the lawyer to join him for a drink in the Grassmarket, where they stayed for hours drinking, eating, laughing and discussing the various similarities and differences between Dunfermline folk and Edinburgh folk. Eventually though time came to pay the bill and, drunk as he was, Duncan still employed his usual tactics and left, leaving Andrew to pay the not unsubstantial bill.

Duncan staggered outside, the fresh air adding to his confusion and, not knowing where he was or where he was going, he wandered for hours until eventually he reached a glassworks in Leith. Finding one of the doors open, he staggered in and threw himself down in a quiet corner beside a furnace, where he fell into a deep sleep.

He was still fast asleep when in the morning the workers arrived and lit the furnace, which was soon stoked into a fierce glaring red heat, large flames shooting out with every blow of the roaring bellows and flashes of vivid light from time to time lighting up the dark space all around. The workmen were busy running about with masses of red-hot molten glass on the end of tubes like demons engaged in some mysterious rituals.

During this time, the workers went as unnoticed by Duncan as he was by them. Eventually though he began to show signs of waking up, rolling about as if in a dreadful nightmare. And indeed he was, as his dreams had brought to mind all his misdeeds, dishonesty and wickedness. All the times he had given short measure, sold damaged linen and, of course, his habit of 'singing the cobbler'. His conscience told him he deserved a terrible punishment. The roaring of the furnace soon brought him to full wakefulness and the sight that met his eyes filled him with unspeakable terror. The noise of the bellows, the fiery red flames leaping from the furnace, the half-naked workers rushing about with their burning globes caused him to whisper, 'Michty me, mercy on my puir soul! Am I here at last? Is that furnace for me? Is that Satan himself I see at the bellows?' On and on he mumbled, listing all the misdeeds and sins he had committed accompanied by deep groans and moans.

Eventually the mutterings reached the ears of one of the workmen, who looked over and saw the unhappy Duncan lying in the corner. As he listened, he instantly understood the situation and saw that the man had wandered into the glassworks in a drunken muddled state and now believed he was in Hell. He shared the knowledge with his fellow workers and the son of the owner and between them they decided to have some amusement at the weaver's expense.

The owner's son, a tall young man, took on the role of the Devil and held up his hand, crying out with a voice of authority, 'Where is the weaver who died in the act of cheating the public and leaving his companions to pay the tavern bill? Where is the scarlet villain that we may roast him in the flames of our ever-burning furnace?'

Duncan lay trembling with terror as the workers approached him, jeering, hooting and yelling, flaming brands in their hands.

'Mercy me, I'm in for it noo!' whispered poor Duncan to himself. 'Please, your glorious Honour and Majesty,' he said in a voice quivering with terror, 'I am Duncan Shulebred, who in the upper world was a puir weaver in the toun o' Dunfermline. I did your honour some sma' service and hope ye winnae be sae hard on me as ye threaten. Keep they awfu' devils frae me and I'll confess to ye a' my crimes! Be mercifu' to a puir sinner!'

'What service did you ever do me?' asked the owner's son.

'I did all that was in my power to get the folk in the upper world to drink wi' me till they were so blind drunk that ye micht hae easily run awa wi' them. Oh, think o' that sir and save me frae that awfu' furnace.'

So Duncan confessed his sins but his tormentors, not satisfied that he had confessed all, picked the terrified man up and began to carry him towards the furnace. Duncan screamed for mercy and all at once seemed as if he would faint. At this point his tormentors called a halt, laid him down and poured some of Duncan's own whisky into his mouth. This seemed to revive him and he sat up, pale, haggard and trembling. He watched as the chief actor filled a glass of spirits and offered it to him. Slowly it dawned on him that he had been made a fool of. Was he furious? In fact, he wasn't.

'You've done mair for me, gentlemen, than all the sermons I ever heard preached in Scotland. I have confessed all my crimes and I will try to make amends for the future. From this moment I will be a sober and upright man and I will try to benefit those whom I have cheated.' And so he did. He sought out Andrew Gavin and repaid the money he had paid for the damaged cloth and settled the bill from the tavern. He resolved never again to taste drink, to get rid of his short ellwand and in what remained of his future life to be honest and just in all his transactions.

THE LEGEND OF THE LADY OF BALWEARIE

Said to date from the sixteenth century, this legend was published in 1860 in the form of a ballad. It tells of how a monk, banished from Balwearie when the laird disposed of lands belonging to the Church, came back one stormy night to the castle and, in front of the lady of the house, pronounced a terrible curse on the house and family:

> 'My curse be now upon this house,
> And on that bairn beside you.
> Deserted be the Bowers
> And empty be the towers
> Of the Castle of Balwearie.
> Who spoils the Kirk will spoiled be,
> Grim vengeance down shall bear you.
> The name of Scott shall be forgot,
> In the Castle o' Balwearie.'

The wind was howling as he went on his way, only to die
near the castle in the rough weather. But his curse remained
and came all too true. The 'bairn', the only son and heir, soon
became ill and died, leaving the lady lamenting:

> 'How can I be but dull today?
> How can I be but drearie?
> I once was glad, but now am sad,
> In the Castle o' Balwearie.'

A second, much more macabre version of the legend exists, also
in ballad form. In this grim tale, Lady Scott of Balwearie com-
missioned a builder named Lambkin to build a second tower
for her to use as a summerhouse. She refuses to pay him for his
work and the disappointed builder approaches her husband.

> It's Lamkin was a mason good as ever built wi' stane;
> He built Lord Wearie's castle but payment got he nane.
> O pay me, Lord Wearie, come pay me my fee,
> I canna pay you Lamkin for I maun gang o'er the sea.

Lamkin curses the family and warns Lord Scott that he will be sorry for not paying up. Despite this threat and the curse, Lord Scott merely tells his lady to keep Lamkin out of the castle and then sails away. A treacherous nurse, however, lets Lamkin in through a little window and reveals that all the men are working in the fields, the women washing at the well and her mistress is sewing in her room, so she alone is in charge of the bairn. On hearing this Lamkin takes a sharp knife and stabs the child in its cradle and then begins to rock it, while the nurse sings, until the blood runs from every hole in the cradle:

> Then Lamkin he rocked and the false nurse sang,
> Till frae ilka bore o' the cradle the red bluid out sprang.

The lady calls down to ask why her son is crying and the nurse lures her into an encounter with Lamkin, who asks, 'O shall I kill her, nurse, or shall I let her be?' only to receive the casual vindictive answer; 'O kill her, kill her Lamkin, for she ne'er was guid tae me.'

The deed was done, but three months later when Lord Scott returns and sees the bloodstains of his wife and child on the floor, retribution follows. The nurse is burned at the stake and Lamkin condemned to death by being locked in the tower and starved.

Legend has it that it was commonplace in the area around Kirkcaldy for the villain, Lamkin, to be used as a nursery 'bogeyman' to terrify children into good behaviour.

FISHER WILLIE

Sir William Anster stayed in Dreel Castle in Anstruther and had interests in herring fishing. He was known familiarly as 'Fisher Willie'. A neighbouring laird, whose estate had the curious name of 'Third-part' presumably after the division of a larger estate sometime in the past, invited Sir William to dinner. What Sir William didn't know was that once he was under the roof of his neighbour the plan was to kill him. It so happened that a tramp took shelter at the Third-part the night before the intended murder. This traveller overheard the laird plotting with his servants and immediately went to warn Sir William. Hearing the plan, Sir William sent a message to excuse himself from the dinner. The Laird of Anster asked the Laird of Third-part to come to Dreel instead. The Laird of Third-part agreed and at the appointed time arrived at Dreel Castle, accompanied by so large an armed retinue that it was obvious that his disappointment was to be made up for with open violence. As he was climbing the narrow spiral staircase of Dreel Castle, Fisher Willie cut him down with a blow from his poleaxe.

The question now arose of how Sir William could win pardon for his deed. Only the King could pardon him. He had to mortgage a great deal of his property in order to buy suitable clothes for his court appearance. He came before the King, declaring that he had the whole of the lands of Anster on his back and could he have permission to continue to wear them. He confessed to having killed the Laird of Third-part and told of the plot overheard. The King, seeing that the motive was clearly self-defence, pardoned him and the family was granted a coat of arms with a poleaxe for their crest. Fisher Willie's coat was said to have been preserved at Ely House, a later residence of the Anstruther family. It was described by those who saw it as being a most voluminous garment with cuffs turned up almost to the shoulder and so stiff with lace as to be almost able to stand on its own. Unfortunately, in the early nineteenth century it was cut down into shreds by a capricious lady and destroyed.

FECHTIN' WHISKY

There once was a publican who lived in the neighbourhood of Dunfermline. He was noted for his quaint humour and his selection of old whisky, of which he would quietly boast that he had in his house all the different kinds of whisky you could wish for: 'bragging whisky,' 'singing whisky', and also the 'fechtin' whisky'. There was a great deal of truth in this as well because if we are observant we may see how very differently affected some people are compared to others when under the influence of strong drink, especially whisky.

Well, one Saturday evening this publican's tavern was full. It was market day and miners, labourers, farmworkers and sailors were all drinking their fill. As the night wore on the company got louder until a great quarrel arose amongst them. There was loud swearing, arguing and fighting going on. So much so that the poor innkeeper was sure it would at least end in bloodshed, if not in the inn being pulled down about his ears. He well knew from long experience that there was no point attempting to reason with such a band of unruly, half-drunken excited men, he would only come off the worst. No, he would have to try strategy, so he went outside to make a plan.

Without a moment's warning he flung the door wide open and went boldly into their midst, brandishing his walking stick over his head.

'Stop, men, stop!' he shouted at the top of his voice. 'For goodness sake stop! Sit down! It's all my fault; it's me that's done all this mischief! I've given you the wrong kind of whisky! I've given you by mistake the fechtin' whisky but if you all sit down quietly I'll bring you in a jug of the very best singing whisky!'

The effect was magical. Peace was immediately restored as he brought in more whisky and began to fill their glasses. Soon the rafters were ringing not with shouts and threats but with songs and laughter and afterwards the company quietly dispersed.

6

SIMPLE FOLK
AND FOOLS

The exploits of foolish and eccentric folk make good stories and here we see that Fife was not short of such people. Some may have existed, some maybe not, but nevertheless their goings-on made for a grand tale to be told round the fireside on a cold night.

WISE WILLIE AND WITTY EPPY

In the county of Fife on the sea coast there stands a little town inhabited by fisherfolk called Buckey Harbour or Buckhaven. Some say the population were sons of fishermen from Norway, who, in a violent storm, were blown over the North Sea and washed ashore here where they settled. Legend has it that they kept to themselves and had little communication with the country folk. Mothers were said to exclaim that they would rather see their bairns dashed against the Bass Rock than see them married to a 'muck-a-byre's' son or daughter.

Wise Willie and Witty Eppy the ale wife lived there about a hundred years ago. Eppy's alehouse was their college and their court where disputes were resolved and puzzles solved and explained. The inn was like a little kirk with four windows and a gable door. The local fishwives got leave to argue as much as they would like as long as it didn't come to blows. Fighting was prohibited. They had no need for minister and kirk or magistrate and courthouse, Witty Eppy and Wise Willie settled all disputes and were rulers of the town.

It happened one day that two fishwives found a horseshoe near the town and brought it to Willie to find out what it was. Willie looked at it and said, 'Indeed, it's a thing with holes in it, where did you find it?'

'Beneath the sky,' they replied.

'Of course!' said Willy. 'It's the auld moon. I ken by the holes in it for nailing it up. But I wonder that it fell in Fife because the last time I saw her she was hanging on her back above Edinburgh. Oh well, we'll set it on the highest house in town and we'll have moonlight of our own every night of the year.'

The whole town came to see the moon but Witty Eppy called out, 'You're all fools together. It's just one of they things the mare wears on her hoof.'

Another time another fishwife found a hare with a broken leg lying amongst the kale in her garden. Not knowing what it was she called for her neighbours to come and see it. Some said it was a gentleman's cat, some a lady's lap dog or a sheep's kitten because it had soft horns. 'Na, na,' cried Willie. 'It's one of they maukins that gentleman's dogs worry.'

'What will we do with it?' they asked.

'We could singe the wool off it and make a sauce for it,' was one suggestion.

'No,' said Eppy, 'we should stick an iron rod through its middle and run round the fire till it's roasted.'

Once, on a dark winter's morning, two of the fishwives were going to Dysart to sell their fish and on the way at the side of the road there happened to be a tinker's donkey with red teeth.

The poor animal, seeing the two wives coming with their creels, thought it was the tinkers coming back for it so it started to bray. The two wives got such a fright that they threw the fish away and ran home crying that they'd seen the horned Devil and it had spoken to them, though they didn't understand what he said.

The whole town was in an uproar. Some wanted to go and attack him with spades and picks. Others wanted to catch him in a strong net then either hang him or drown him. 'No, no,' said Wise Willie. 'We don't need to fall out with him. He's got the two creels of fish. He'll go on his way and not bother us anymore. Anyway, he's too supple to be caught in a net and your spirit will neither hang him nor drown him and where he comes from, well, he's used to the heat so he's not going to burn. We'll go to him in a civil manner and see what he wants. Get Witty Eppy and Nancy and tell them to bring their bible and psalm book.'

So off they went in a crowd either to kill the Devil or catch him alive. As they came near, the donkey started to bray louder than ever, which caused some to faint and others to run away.

'No, no, no,' shouted Willie, 'that's no the De'il's words at all. It's a heavenly trumpeter blowing on his brass whistle!' Willie crept forward till he could see the donkey's two lugs. 'Now,' said Willie, 'come forward and hold him fast. I can see his two horns.' So they surrounded the poor animal on all sides, still thinking it was the Devil, but when Wise Willie saw that the beast didn't have cloven feet he cried out, 'This is no the De'il, it's some living beast, neither cow nor horse.'

'What is it then Willie?' he was asked.

'Indeed,' answered Willie, 'it's the faither o' they maukins. I ken by its lang lugs.'

Another time a gentleman coming past the town asked one of the fishwives where the college was. 'Gie me a shilling and I'll show ye baith sides o't.' she answered.

He gave her a shilling, thinking he was about to be shown something curious.

'Now,' she says, 'there's one side of the shilling and there's the other, so now it's mine.'

There was a custom in Buckey Harbour that, after a heavy drinking session, they would go down to dance amongst the boats. One day they allowed gly'd Rob, who was a warlock, to join them and he made them all stop their dancing. For this he was hauled before Wise Willie, who had him banished to the Isle of May to carry coals to the lighthouse.

So this Buckhaven was once noted for droll exploits and some say this history is too ironic, but it is as it is according to the knowledge of the times. The old wives will tell you yet of the Devil appearing to their grandparents and dead wives visiting their families long after being buried.

STEWED TEA

Grizel Millar, owner of the earliest tavern and brewery in St Monans, often held special celebrations in the inn, especially on the occasion of her foster daughter's birthday. One time as a novel present for the guests, she was given a pound of tea by a seafaring nephew of the laird. This luxury had only been introduced recently to the country and what she should do with it presented a real puzzle to the elderly Grizel. But she wasn't to be baffled by this new-fangled thing, after all, was she not famed for her splendid soup?

So on goes the pot and in goes the pound of tea with quite a bit of water because she thought that it would require a great deal of boiling. As she stirred the pot she noticed a gradual expansion of the leaves, which led her to congratulate herself on her 'tea cooking' skills.

But soon, seeing that the tea was growing so much that it was in danger of spilling out of the pot, she changed her mind about what she should do and poured out the water, which she admitted to herself had a terrible colour.

Then to the pot she added butter, spice and minced onions, causing the novel 'stew' to give off rather an unusual smell. A little more spice was added and the dish was ready to be given pride of place on the table surrounded by haggis, a pile of bannocks and a flagon of ale.

Now everyone who has ever been involved in the preparation of a special celebration will know of the anxiety and stress experienced so will readily sympathise with Grizel when she decided to rest her weary bones and dispense with being hostess that evening and not to greet the guests on arrival.

In her place came Uncle Bob. Now Uncle Bob was a seafaring man, a loud and boastful seafaring man but well capable of playing 'Mine Host'. But he also liked his ale and all the while he was welcoming the guests and regaling them with boastful tales of his exploits at sea he was eyeing up the table, especially the flagon of ale. Not wanting to immediately begin drinking, he invited the guests to begin eating by first taking a spoonful of the haggis and then he had a swig of the ale, then a bit of the bannock and another swig of ale, all the time praising his niece's cooking skills. Then he took a spoonful of the unusual 'stewed tea' and swallowed, a grimace quickly replacing the grin on his face. Afterwards he nearly drained the flagon of ale before inviting the guests to 'dig in', still praising his niece. It's not recorded what the guests thought of the unusual 'stew' but there is no record of it having become a local delicacy.

A Pig in a Poke

In days gone by it was customary for parishioners to contribute in kind to the upkeep of their minister. A young Dunfermline minister who had been given a wee pig found that the cost of feeding it was getting expensive as it grew so he decided to send it to a friend who stayed at Cairneyhill. This friend had ample room for it and would give it free board and lodging for a while. It was customary in those days to transport pigs in a poke or sack, so he put the pig in a sack and asked his beadle to take it to Cairneyhill. Now, the beadle had a bit of a reputation for being a blether and for not being very bright, so the minister impressed on him that he was to tell no one where he was going and what was in the sack. He didn't want his parishioners to know.

The beadle assured the minister he wouldn't say a word about his errand and away he trudged with the precious bundle on his back.

Down the road a bit he arrived at Crossford, where he came across three acquaintances who were standing by the door of the inn.

'What you got there?' they shouted to him.

He told them that he daren't tell what he was carrying nor where he was going but he could tell them that it was neither a dog nor a cat.

The young men said they would ask no more, but then they kindly suggested he might like to join them for a wee dram as he would be tired with his journey and his burden. He tried to refuse, saying that he couldn't well go into the inn because the minister would never trust him with 'a pig in a poke' again, not thinking what he had said.

However, the young men were persuasive and decent and kind-looking so eventually the beadle agreed to leave the sack

at the door for just a minute and join them for the 'mouthful' kindly offered. As soon as he had stepped inside, one of the young men opened the sack and pulled out the pig, replacing it with a wee black dog. The guileless beadle, not suspecting a thing, finished his dram and set off cheerily on his journey again, soon delivering his burden to the minister's friend.

The beadle's face was a picture when he opened the sack and found not a pig but a wee black dog. The poor beadle yelled in alarm. 'The De'il's surely been busy since I left the manse. He's turned the pig from white tae black!'

The minister's friend was also bewildered at the sight and told the beadle to take the dog back to the minister again, as he had no use for it.

'It's no a dog sir, it's a pig that Satan himself has turned from white to black!' He then very ruefully put the dog back in the sack and carefully tied it up again before setting out on his return journey.

He soon passed the inn door again, where he saw the three young men standing quietly and innocently by the door. He told them where he had been and what dreadful thing had happened to the minister's pig. They sympathized and seemed as much astonished at the tale as he was. They suggested that he join them once again in the inn for a wee rest and maybe a wee dram to set him up for the rest of the journey, which he was tempted to do. This time the dog was taken from the sack and the pig returned.

The unsuspecting beadle trudged back to the manse, many strange and gruesome thoughts passing through his muddled brain. He told the minister of the day's disaster and that his Cairneyhill friend had insisted he bring the sack back immediately. The minister was much perplexed and greatly annoyed by the tale and asked the beadle to untie the sack and put the pig back in the sty.

'It's no a pig, sir! It's a wee black dog; I'll let you see for yourself!' He opened the sack and let out an almighty screech as the pig stuck its snout out.

And the minister? Well he was completely confused by the beadle's strange tale and didn't know what to think.

THE FUDDLED TALE OF KIND KYTTOCK

Kyttock wasn't originally from Fife. No, she came from the other side of the Forth, a place called Little France, just south of Edinburgh, so-called because some of the ladies Mary Queen of Scots brought from France were lodged there.

Kyttock came to Fife and settled in Falkland as the young bride of a falconer at the palace. She was a bonnie, lively lassie if a little flighty, as was many a lass from Little France who copied Queen Mary's ladies.

Her first tasks as a new wife were to arrange her wee home and to learn the likes and dislikes of her big, slow man and work out what she should change for the sake of comfort.

Then she bore his bairns, a lassie and seven braw laddies, all with jet black hair like their father. She buried three and steered the rest to adulthood, seeing them wed with good tochers of fine linen and pewter plate. She worked hard, scrubbing and cooking, stitching and stoking. She fed her cats, tended her garden and a few chickens. She was first to knock on a door when she heard someone was in trouble and quick to offer passers-by refreshment. Yet in all her busy life, as she aged and her back grew bent, she was still the bonnie, honest lassie her man had married, with a smooth complexion and always a fresh white cap on her head. And she was kind.

In fact, she was so near perfect that the good folk of Falkland were as sure as Kyttock herself that the one failing she did have wouldn't keep her from the gates of Heaven when her time came.

For Kyttock did have one failing, a great thirst for the ale. Folk said she could out-drink the menfolk at the inn and still toddle back to her own kitchen in time to have her man's supper on the table when he got home from work. They say it's what you love the best that gets you in the end. Well Kyttock loved a lot of thing as well as the ale … her man, her bairns and grand-bairns, her garden and her fellow Falklanders. But if that saying is true then the ale must have had a wee edge over the others, for it was at the end of a sunny afternoon, amongst the daisies in her garden and with an empty keg by her side, that Kyttock gently keeled over and went fearlessly to meet her maker.

The dwam that she died in must have still been on her for her mind was in a rare old fuddle as she set off on the Highway to Heaven. She had a strange feeling that she strayed off the path to a fairy well, where there was only plain water to drink and no signpost to show her the way. She dozed a while by the well then blinked herself awake. Sure now that she wasn't dreaming, she looked about her and spotted a snail, aye a snail, squeezing and stretching its way past her.

'Guid snail, dae ye ken the road tae St Peter's yett?' she asked.

'I'm makin' ma wey there noo. Best hurry efter me,' answered the snail. She wasn't too fuddled to have a laugh at that.

'I'll keep up with you even if you run a hundred times faster,' she replied.

They set off, and a right pair they looked, the snail with his shell and Kyttock with her bent back, shuffling along like echoes, until it got dark. They still hadn't reached the gates but they had reached an alehouse, which looked not unlike the inn at Falkland. There the snail left her.

'Just half a mile up the road tomorrow and you'll be there,' he said as he hunched away. Kyttock wasn't hungry but the old thirst was there. That evening she drank deep of the inn's brew and though time meant nothing now, she slept until what in Falkland would have been noon the next day. She hurried towards the Pearly Gates, a bit ashamed that she had lost her way yesterday. She hid a while behind a pillar and when St Peter had his back turned she slipped through. Now that gave the Good Lord a right laugh, better than he'd laughed since the sixth day when his creating was done. He'd looked down over the years on Kyttock, noting her skills in the garden and the house, and all her kind ways with the neighbours, so he made her the under-hen wife.

For seven earthly years Kyttock lived a virtuous life, mainly because the ale in Heaven was sour and didn't tempt her away from her near perfection; near perfection because they say that St Peter never forgave her for managing to dodge past him and every time they met they fell to arguing. Then one fateful day, when she wandered near the gates, with the hens scratching round her feet, she caught sight of the alehouse up the road and all of a sudden she was gripped by a longing for a long, cool draught of ale. She forgot the hens and the seven virtuous years, and again slipped past St Peter, making her way to the inn. There she sat in the garden amongst the daisies, with two cats at her feet, happily quenching her thirst.

And that was that. St Peter wasn't going to be caught a third time and sternly stopped her when she returned a little unsteadily that night. He clipped her round the ears and sent her back to the inn for all eternity.

There she took up something not unlike her old life in Falkland, cleaning, baking, sweeping, and pouring out pitchers of ale for passers-by. So when one by one her family and friends joined her en-route to Heaven, what with the chores, the daisies, the cats and the ale, she was never quite sure where she was.

STRUNTY POKES

There was once a man who liked to have everything different from other people and when he hired a manservant he made him promise to call everything by the queer names he invented.

'Now, John,' he said, 'when you speak to me what will you call me?'

'Why, sir,' said John, 'I'll call you Master, or Your Honour, or anything else you like!'

'No, John, that won't do. You must call me Master above all masters. And what will you call my house?'

'I'll call it your house, your mansion, or what you please.'

'No, that'll no do. You must call it Mount Aupris. And now what will you call my wife?'

'I'll call her Mistress, or Your Lady, or anything else you please, sir,' said John, who was really quite an obliging man.

'No,' said his master, 'you must call her Dumbalibus. And what will you call the fire?'

'Just the fire I suppose,' said John.

'No,' said the gentleman, 'you must call it the great flame of light. And now, what will you call my trousers?'

'Well, sir, I'll call them your trousers, your breeches, or whatever you like.'

'You must call them my strunty pokes, John,' said the master, 'and then what will you call my cat?'

'Oh, just Pussy or Kitty, or anything you choose,' was the answer.

'No, you must call it the Great man of Crayantis. And what will you call the water?'

'Oh, just water,' said John, who couldn't think of any other word for it.

'No,' said the master, 'you must call it Gillipontis.'

Well, the servant did his best to remember these names to please his strange master, and he soon became so used to them that he could say them just as easily as the old ones. So one night when the man and the cat were sitting at the kitchen fire a cinder fell out and, as luck would have it, it fell upon the cat's tail and set it on fire. Then what a to-do there was, as it ran squealing up the stairs in a terrible fright, setting fire to everything on its way. The master was by this time in bed, so the servant rushed to his room and beat on his door crying out: 'Wake up Master above all masters, waken Dumbalibus and put on your strunty pokes. The Great man of Crayantis has gone up to the top of Mount Aupris and if we don't get some help from Gillipontis we shall all be burnt to death!'

JOHNNY TROTTER

There was once a farmer and his wife from Fife, Johnny and Jean Trotter. They wanted to plant seed in their field but they didn't have the money for it, so they decided to sell their cow at market and spend the money on seed. Johnny was to drive it into town but when it came to it, Jean decided she didn't trust him not to spend the money on drink, so she set off herself with the cow and a hen besides.

On the way she met a butcher, who asked, 'Will you sell that cow Gudewife?'

'Aye, I will,' she answered. 'I'll be wanting five shillings for it and you can have the hen too for ten pounds.'

'Very good,' said the man. 'I don't want the hen, you'll get rid of it easy enough in town, but I'll have the cow for five shillings.'

She sold him the cow but no one in town wanted the hen either, so she went back to the butcher and said, 'I can't get rid of this hen. You took the cow so you must take it too.'

'Well,' said the butcher, 'we'll see about that.' He treated her to food and drink and gave her so much brandy that she lost her head and fell fast asleep. While she slept, the butcher dipped her in a tar barrel and then laid her on a heap of feathers. When she woke up she was covered in feathers and didn't know what had happened to her.

'Is it me, or is it not me? No it can't be me; it must be some great strange bird. But how do I find out? I know, I'll be able to tell when I get home if the calves come and lick me and the dog doesn't bark.'

But the dog, when he saw her, set up such a barking that you would have thought all the robbers in the world were in the yard.

'Aw dearie me,' said Jean, 'it can't be me, I thought so.'

So she went to the byre where the calves were but they wouldn't lick her when they smelled the tar.

'Oh no, it can't be me. It must be some strange bird.' So she crept up on the roof and began to flap her arms as if she was about to fly. When Johnny Trotter saw all this, out he came with his gun and he began to take aim at her.

'Oh, don't shoot,' cried his wife. 'I think it's only me!'

'If it is you,' he said, 'don't stand up there like a cow on a roof, come down here and let me hear what you have to say for yourself.' So she crawled back down, but she hadn't a shilling to show for the money she got from the butcher because she had thrown it away in her drunkenness. When her husband heard her story he said, 'You're only twice as daft as you were before,' and he got so angry that he decided to leave her altogether and never come back till he had found three other wives as daft as his.

Off he went and when he'd walked a wee bit he saw a gude-wife running in and out of a wooden house with a sieve and every time she ran in she threw her apron over the sieve, just as if she had something in it, and when she got inside she turned it upside down on the floor. 'What are you doing?' he asked.

'I'm only carrying in a wee bit of sun, but I don't know how it is that outside I have the sun in my sieve but when I get inside somehow I've thrown it away. But in my old cottage I had plenty of sun and I never had to carry any. If I knew someone who would bring the sun in I would give him a bag of gold.'

So Johnny Trotter asked for an axe and cut windows in the cottage because the builder had forgotten them. The sun shone in and he got his gold.

'That was one,' he said to himself as he went on his way. After a while he passed another house. What a screaming and yelling was coming from it. So he went in and saw a gudewife hard at work banging her husband over the head with a mallet. Over the man's head was a shirt without any slit for his neck.

'Why are you beating your gudeman to death?' he asked.

'I'm not,' she replied. 'I just need to make a hole in the shirt for his neck.' All the time the gudeman was screaming and calling out, 'If anyone could just teach my wife another way of making a slit for my neck in my new shirts I'd give them a bag of gold.'

'I'll do it if you just give me a pair of shears.' He got scissors and snipped a hole in the neck and got his bag of gold.

'That's another one,' he said to himself as he walked on.

Last of all he came to a farm where he decided to rest for a bit. When he went in the gudewife asked him where he came from.

'Oh! I come from Paradise Place,' he said, because that was the name of his farm.

'Paradise Place? Then you must know my second husband, Peter, who is dead and gone to Paradise?'

'Oh aye, I know him well.'

'So how do things go with him?' she asked.

'Only middling,' was the answer. 'He goes about begging from house to house and has neither food nor rag to his back. As for money he hasn't a sixpence to his name.'

'Mercy me, he never should go about like that when he left so much behind. Why there are clothes upstairs and a chest full of money. If you were to take them with you when you go back to Paradise, I'd give you a horse and cart to carry them.'

So Johnny got a cartload of clothes and a chest full of money and as much food and drink as he could eat.

'Well that was the third,' he said to himself as he jumped on the cart and rode off.

Now this gudewife's new husband was ploughing a field nearby when he saw the man driving away from the farm with his horse and cart, so he rushed home.

'Who was that?'

'Oh him! He was from Paradise and he said my second man is in a poor way, so I sent him all those old clothes he left behind and the chest of money.'

On hearing this the husband saddled his horse and road off after the cart at full gallop. It wasn't long before he was close behind the cart but he was seen and Johnny Trotter drove the cart into a thicket by the side of the road. Pulling a handful of hair from the horse's tail he jumped up into a birch tree and tied it to a branch then lay down under the tree, peering up at the sky.

'Well, well,' he said as the husband rode up. 'I never saw the like of this in all my days.'

The husband looked up, wondering what he was looking at.

'I never did see anything like it. Here is a man going straight to heaven on a black horse. You can see the tail still hanging on the branch and up there you can see the black horse.'

'I don't see anything but the horsehair in the birch.'

'No you wouldn't. You'll have to lie down here and stare at the sky.'

So he lay down and stared at the sky till his eyes began to sting and fill with water. Meanwhile Johnny Trotter jumped on the horse and rode off with both it and the horse and cart.

When he reached home with two bags of gold and a cartload of clothes and money he saw all his fields ploughed and sown. The first thing he asked his wife was where she had got the seed from.

'Oh!' she said. 'I have always heard that what a man does sow he shall reap, so I sowed the salt which our friends laid up here with us and if we get some rain I fancy it will come up nicely.'

'Daft you are,' said Johnny Trotter, 'and daft you will be so long as you live, but that's all one now for the rest are not a bit wiser than you. There's not a pin to choose between you.'

STUCK IN THE LUM

Pattiesmuir near Dunfermline, like many small villages in Fife, could boast of having many bonnie lassies within its borders. Their fame was known far and wide to the country lads. It happened that one such lad who lived some miles away took a fancy to one of these bonnie lassies. His courtship progressed smoothly and favourably despite the disadvantage that the father and mother of the lassie were very strict in all their ways.

One evening the young lad was somewhat later than usual in getting away from his farm work and when he arrived at the humble cottage of his love he was disappointed to find, despite the fact that she was expecting him that evening, the family had all retired to bed. In those quiet-going, candle-saving times, when daylight was so precious, the maxim in all well-ordered families used to be, 'Early to bed and early to rise'.

In this cottage the evening's family worship (which was common in most families) was past and silence reigned in the house. While the young man miserably surveyed first the back and then the front of the cottage which housed his dearest love, the sentiments contained in an old song came over him:

> Her father he has locked the door,
> Her mother keeps the key;
> But neither door nor bolt shall part
> My own true love from me!

He had travelled many miles that cold night to see his sweetheart and great was his disappointment. What could he do? Was he to make his weary way back home and come again another evening? Would she be sitting alone by the kitchen fire thinking of him? These were the questions which occupied his thoughts. After some consideration a bright idea flashed into his mind and he resolved to carry it out because in his frame of mind he knew that 'love laughs at locksmiths'.

It had occurred to him that, rather than go home without seeing her and rather than disturb the family by knocking on the door he would climb on the roof of the cottage, which would not be in the least bit difficult. He could then go quietly down the inside of the lum to the kitchen. And any inconvenience arising from getting covered in soot would easily be remedied by a good shake. So up onto the roof he went, over the roof and into the lum. Then he began to cautiously descend. The top of the chimney was wider than he had expected but as he descended he found that it got alarmingly narrow. Coming to a bend he got completely STUCK! He twisted and turned and turned and twisted but despite this exertion he found he could get neither up nor down. Here was a dilemma; a thoughtless disreputable piece of luck for him, a decent country lad. He was completely confined on all sides and covered completely over with sweat and soot. Desperate, he was at last compelled to shout for assistance. This brought some of the drowsy villagers to the cottage but there was some trouble at first in ascertaining where the strange shouts were coming from. They looked east and the looked west but the sounds at first seemed near then far.

They fell on the ears of the villages like the strange notes of the cuckoo which can be distinctly heard yet the bird itself is usually invisible or at least rarely seen. The extraordinary situation and circumstances soon dawned on them and became apparent in time. There was nothing for it but to take down a portion of the chimney and gable of the house to relieve the lad's suffering. A handy labourer was found and the prisoner was set free. His sad sooty appearance did nothing to endear him in the eyes of his lady-love and her family, nor were they and the bystanders impressed by his good sense and wisdom. So the poor lad slunk home, the butt of jokes and stories for many a day.

THE GUDEWIFE OF AUCHTERMUCHTY

There once was a farmer and his wife who had a farm in Auchtermuchty. They were a hardworking couple, the wife keeping the house and looking after the animals while the gudeman worked in the fields from dawn to dusk. One day he came home soaked to the skin, having been ploughing all day in the kind of rain and wind field-workers in Fife often have to endure. Seeing his wife sitting spinning by a warm fire, her day's work done, he said, 'Aye wife, I think maybe we should change places tomorrow. I'll look after the house; you have a day in the fields.'

'Aye,' she says, 'I'll agree to that. But mind, by the time I finish you'll need to have the bairns bedded, the dough kneaded, the butter churned, the cows and the geese herded, and the kiln kindled.'

Well, the next day all goes well with the wife's ploughing. At the end of the day she unharnessed the nine oxen from the common plough of the village and made her way home.

But things haven't gone so well with the gudeman.

First he went out to feed the geese but found a greedy hawk had helped itself to all but two of the seven goslings. Then he wanted to churn the butter because they had to have butter for supper. But when he had churned a while he felt thirsty so went down to the cellar to open a barrel of ale so he could have a drink. When he had knocked out the bung and was putting the tap into the cask he heard the pig come into the kitchen above. Off he ran up the steps as fast as he could with the tap still in his hand to stop the pig knocking over the churn, but when he got there he saw the pig had already knocked it over and was standing grunting amongst the cream, which was running all over the floor. He got wild with rage and completely forgot the ale-barrel and ran at the pig as hard as he could. He caught it just as it was running out of the door and gave it such a kick that it dropped dead on the spot, killing the remaining two goslings in the process.

Then he remembered the tap in his hand so he ran down into the cellar again but when he got there he saw that every drop of ale had run out of the cask.

He went back into the dairy and found enough cream left to fill the churn again. He churns and churns for over an hour until the sweat's pouring off him but only gets a sorrowfully wee pat of butter for his trouble.

Then he remembers the milking cow is still shut up in the byre and hasn't had a drop to eat or drink all morning. When he tries to drive it out the bad-tempered beast stabs him in the arm with its horn.

Next he tries spinning but gets himself in a right tangle with the yarn, so he puts the pot on the fire but forgets to put in the water and the fire burns the bottom out of it. He goes to kindle the kiln but puts too much wood on and it blazes up.

Next he puts the bairns to bed but they've been paddling in the burn and dirty the sheets. He tries to wash the sheets in the burn but it is in spate and the sheets get carried away.

At this point he puts his head in his hands and shakes his head.

'Aye,' he says, 'I should have stayed with the ploughing; me and the hoose will never dae weel. A man jist cannae dae the work of a woman.'

7

TALES IN THE LANDSCAPE

BUFF BAREFOOT

One night a tall dark figure wrapped in a black cloak, his face concealed by a hood, was seen carrying a basket on the road from Newark Castle to St Monans. The season was winter. There was no moon. The only light was that of the stars shining on the sea. He deviated neither to the left nor the right till he reached his destination. The basket was left on the doorstep of the tavern near the harbour kept by a certain Grizel Miller, the first brewer and innkeeper to have existed in Netherton of St Monans. The figure rapped on the door and having done so, disappeared into the gloom.

Grizel had been expecting some supplies for her house so thought that the covered basket contained these, but hearing the visitor retreat called out, 'Wait! I'll get you your baw-bees.' Getting no answer she plucked the basket from the steps, locked the door once again and set it down in a corner of the kitchen. It was late, so she didn't look inside right away but sat down by the fire, thinking it seemed strange that the messenger hadn't waited. All was quiet except for the crackling of the logs in the fire. Suddenly she heard a strange noise and she imagined she saw something move in the shadows where the flames of the fire flickered on the wall. The supernatural was always lurking on the edges of folk's minds in those days so Grizel called fearfully to her niece who, hearing the tremble in her aunt's voice, came in with an open bible already in her hand.

The shrill cry of an infant came from the basket as she entered.

'Lord be with us lassie, it's a bairn! Do you think it's a fairy changeling?' the old lady asked as she lifted the basket to the table and removed the cover, fearing that the fairies had left one of their imps, despite there being no newborns to take in exchange. But this was no imp! It was a newborn bairn, a fine wee lassie dressed in the best of clothes and with a bag of gold hidden in the blanket.

'In all the wide world what does this mean?' asked Grizel. 'This is no common bairn but probably a mistake of the laird. We'll take the bairn and call it our ain.' So here the matter rested for the night.

The next day the laird from Grangemuir visited the inn as he often did for his amusement because there he was able to catch up on all the goings-on of the district. This time, though, the marvellous basket was all that was being talked about and he listened with intense interest.

'It's a braw fair-skinned bairn, sir, and not that unlike yourself if my een dinna deceive me.'

'Wheest Grizel!', replied the laird. 'You're surely daft!'

'No, sir, I'm not that daft. It has the very same black een that you have.'

'No more of your nonsense. Bring me some ale.'

'Aye, aye,' says Grizel. 'But there's much worse can come to your house than a braw wee bairn, ye ken.'

Grizel was much enamoured with the child and took it upon herself to raise her and keep her from danger both real and imagined by concealing, within the folds of her garments, a huge lammer bead, a bead made of the finest amber, because it is well known in the East Neuk for its mystic ability to protect defenceless children from any fairy influence.

The seasons passed and the little mysterious foundling grew up as fair as a lily, hardy and strong but more genteel than the maids around her. It was noted, almost with surprise, that she followed the practice of the class in which she had been raised by taking a dislike to footwear and going without shoes. What Christian name she was given has been long forgotten but because of this habit, she was known in St Monans as Buff Barefoot.

Seventeen years passed, each year celebrated with a party at the laird's home, Grangemuir House, to which all were invited, common folk and gentry alike. This year after the celebration the girl was returning from helping a much inebriated guest home when a huge Newfoundland dog bounded towards her. At first she shrank with terror from the hound but when it lay down at her feet, gazing at her with its big brown eyes, she realised it meant her no harm. As she reached to stroke it, the dog gently took a hold of her skirt with its teeth and pulled as if saying, 'Come with me.' When it ran off, she followed and then the whole mystery unfolded. A fine ship dashed to pieces on the rocks, the shore strewn with the wreck. The captain, a fine young man and sole survivor of the catastrophe, thrown up on the beach and left so entangled with the wreck by the receding tide as to make it impossible to free himself. The dog ran and licked his face and together girl and dog were able to release the sailor and take him back to her foster mother's home, where he was welcomed and given the necessary treatment his condition needed. It turned out that this mariner was in fact a long lost nephew of Grizel, the family having been scattered to the four corners of the Empire. When he saw the beautiful young girl who had rescued him from certain death, he fell completely in

love with her and Grizel could see that the girl returned that
love. Having been duped by a sailor herself in the past and
having the feeling that this girl, though penniless, was of high
descent and a match for a baron or some other titled suitor,
Grizel arranged for the stranger to go live with her brother.
Here he stayed until his affairs were settled and then because
he had lost everything in the shipwreck he was sent off on a
trading voyage to recoup his lost fortune.

Meanwhile the mansion at Grangemuir was visited by a
distant relative of the laird. This visitor was in fact a border
freebooter who had amassed a fortune by plunder and criminal
acts and who had no conscience or heart. He was introduced to
the beauty of St Monans and Grizel's tavern was much visited
by him so he could meet her. But she refused all his attentions.

The day was now near when the sailor was to return to
claim his bride and the border raider, learning this, determined
to take his place. He discovered how letters came and went
between the lovers then intercepted a message asking Buff to
welcome back her lover in the moonlight beneath St Mary's tree
on the Doocot Hill. She told her foster mother that she was

going to keep the tryst and she did. Scarcely had she time to reach the spot than St Monans was roused by shrieks and pistol shots. The sailor reached the spot first and seeing the figure of a man running off, followed him. The villagers, some still in their nightclothes, found Buff Barefoot dying on the ground and far off in the distance a fleeing figure. He was pursued and, stumbling in the unfamiliar landscape, was overtaken and recognised as the sailor from over the sea. The freebooter was nowhere to be seen. The sailor was taken and locked up in a dungeon at Newark Castle to await his fate. The real villain was eventually overcome with remorse. His wild life in the Borders had troubled him little but now the ghosts of the past peopled his dreams and his waking hours alike, so he confessed before finally finding a suicide's grave.

From the moment of her death the spirit of Buff Barefoot haunted Grangemuir House. Every night the sound of bare feet running through its rooms and along its passages disturbed the sleep of the household. There were some who saw as well as heard. For a century it is said that only those impervious to fear stayed at the mansion. Eventually it was abandoned. Another house was built a little way off but not a scrap of masonry from the old house was used in the building of the new in case the ghost should follow.

The Gold of Tower Hill

If you are brave enough to wander over Tower Hill above Tayport when the clouds are low and the mist thick you might have the misfortune to catch sight of a lantern glimmer as it flits to and fro amongst the heather and bracken. If the dim light of the stars happen to shine through, it is sometimes possible to glimpse the carrier.

Centuries ago they say a local laird, afraid for the safety of his hard-earned gold, the idol of his miserly heart, hid some somewhere on the Muir and some on the hill above Tayport.

The times were troubled. Might often won over right. No banks existed and secure hiding places were hard to find, but the places the laird found would be safe for the time being until he needed to seek it again.

But when he next was able to add to his hoard he couldn't remember the exact spot where he had buried the gold. Everywhere on the Muir and hill looked the same to him. Frantically he searched and dug but he could find nothing but sand, heather, roots and bracken. Night after night, winter after winter, when darkness and solitude favoured his search he returned to the Muir and hillside and his frantic task. Death didn't stop him either. Though the gold he was looking for had probably long turned to dust, he wanders in vain searching still.

The belief in the existence of buried treasure somewhere on the hill is kept alive by an old rhyme:

Here I sit and here I see,
St Andrews, Broughty and Dundee,
And as muckle below me as wad buy a' three
In a kist.

THE LEGEND OF BELL CRAIG

The cave at Bell Craig is reputed to have been one of the sources of power exercised by the Wizard of Balwearie and that what the stars were unable to reveal he discovered by its aid. They say that at times there came from the cave 'an air from heaven or a blast from hell' and if properly inhaled it carried with it the gift of second sight. Travellers whose way took them past the Craig were said to 'experience peculiar sensations', or on wild nights hear an unearthly howling, said to be the coronach played by a spectre piper doomed forever to pay for the misuse of the powers gifted by the unseen presence.

The legend goes that the unfortunate piper, who had been displaying his skill at Lochgelly Fair, was journeying to Kirkcaldy. It was late in the evening when he drew near the Lang Toun. A storm raged and whistled amongst the rocks and trees in the valley of the Tiel. As he passed the Bell Craig a strange sense of exhilaration seized him. He knew the reputation of the cave so he might have asked for the gift to be bestowed, but his senses had been dulled by the precautions taken on his journey past the loch and through the hills by Auchtertool, a road so lonely in those days as to daunt even the bravest soul without a dram or two.

He cared now for neither the seen nor unseen. So instead of pausing in awe and reverence when he felt the strange influence of that place, he defiantly placed the chanter to his lips. Never again in life would he do so. The music, wild and unearthly, rose above the howling of the storm and continued so until dawn. It died with the storm and with the rising of the sun. A farm labourer on his way to the fields discovered the piper stretched dead at the entrance to the cave, the chanter still between his lips.

The Gold of Largo Law

On the northern shores of the Forth estuary stands Largo Law. This striking natural feature is the scene of many legends and was once a site of great ritual importance. One of the stories connected with it has had a hold on local imagination for a very long time. It concerns Largo Law and an ancient tumulus or burial mound a mile to the north, called Norrie's Law.

For hundreds of years it has been said that somewhere deep within the hill is a store of hidden gold. So convinced were the locals that whenever a sheep was seen to have wool tinged with yellow, folk said that it must have been lying above the hoard. It is said that once the Law was haunted by a grim spectre who was condemned to roam the earth until he could pass on the secret of the buried gold. Some folk said he had been a robber, some a pirate, but it had to be spoken to before he would speak the truth. Many had thought of finding him and asking where the gold was, but none had been brave enough.

A shepherd on the nearby farm of Balmain, inspired by an all-powerful love of gold, became obsessed with the hidden treasure and resolved to try and get his hands on it. Nobody had a good word to say about this shepherd and he thought they would think better of him if he was rich.

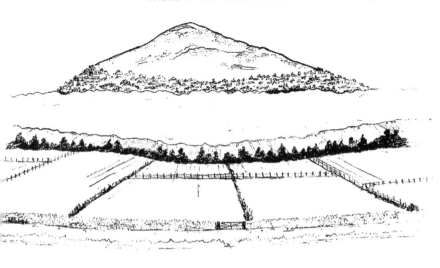

One cold winter's night, after months of roaming the slopes of the Law, he was out again on the hill when he saw some mist on the slopes. Thinking that this at last might be the ghost, he approached with his heart in his mouth. As he did so the mist swilled and became a huge awful-looking spectre. Feeling brave, maybe because he had had a dram or two, just to keep out the cold, he decided to ask where the gold was. Summoning all his willpower he approached the spectre and asked what kept it from its rest and forced it to prowl the slopes of Largo Law night after night when all good folk were fast asleep in their beds.

The spirit looked deep into his eyes, chilling him to the marrow, and then it said:

> 'If Auchendowie cock disnae craw,
> An the herd o' Balmain disnae blaw,
> I'll tell ye whar the gowd is on Largo Law.
> Come here the morn, and dinnae be late,
> For I'll no wait past the hour o' eight.'

The shepherd thought that he now had the gold within his grasp. He wasted not a moment. That night all the cockerels on Auchendowie Farm or within earshot of Largo Law were mysteriously throttled. The following morning the shepherd was up at dawn and ran to Balmain. There he threatened the herdsman Tammie Norrie, telling him not to blow his horn to summon the cattle home that evening on pain of death, pulling aside his coat to show the knife held there.

Having done all he could to fulfil the ghost's conditions, the shepherd could do nothing but wait. At last the appointed hour came and he headed up the Law to meet the ghost. Just as the bogle was about to tell him where the gold was, the unmistakeable sound of a cow horn was heard in the distance. It was Tammie Norrie. Whether by accident or design he had ignored the shepherd's instruction. The shepherd stared, wide-eyed with dismay, as the bogle vanished into nothing and its voice boomed out from the darkness,

> 'Woe to the man who blew that horn,
> For out of that spot he shall ne'er be borne.'

Mad with rage, the disappointed shepherd ran north to have his revenge upon the cowherd. Eventually he reached the spot from where the horn had sounded. He could hardly believe his eyes. There stood Tammie Norrie, horn still at his lips, but turned to stone. The ghost's curse had literally petrified the unfortunate cowherd. Try as they might the local people couldn't move him and eventually they simply heaped a cairn over him which was from then on known as Norrie's Law.

Carlin Maggie and the Devil's Burden

It is said that once, Glen Vale in the Lomond Hills was the chosen haunt of witches. There they hovered, flying up and down the narrow gorge, darting fiendishly and huddling upon the cliffs, devising mischief against mankind. Carlin Maggie was their chosen Queen.

Now it happened one day, as they met in the Glen, a clamour of fright rose in their midst, because some of the witches riding in mid-air had seen the Devil himself approach round the hillside. On his back he carried a great pile of boulders which was greatly slowing him down, but at the alarm, the witches fled. They feared they might not be able to stand up to an evil power superior to their own. Angry, their Queen watched them flee, and then flew above them to land on a rocky outcrop on the Bishop's Hill. There she stood looking out across the glen, shrieking defiantly and taunting loudly the mastermind of mischief.

He listened, amazed and angry too. Suddenly he threw down the boulders from his back and rushed to meet Maggie.

Maggie, with outspread talons, waited his approach eager for confrontation but when he drew closer and she saw the awful Presence face-to-face, the centre of all evil, his eyes ablaze with fury, she changed her mind and fled in the opposite direction. Her impotence confessed to all, she ran along the ledge of the outcrop and, close behind, Satan followed. It was an unequal chase, for soon the Carlin was compelled to yield to her antagonist's superior speed and, upon a lonely point that overlooks tranquil Loch Leven, was forced to pause. At that instant Satan stood before his shrinking foe. He gazed into her eyes and over her head he waved his mighty arm, turning her to stone.

And on that height Carlin Maggie still stands, a stony figure solitary, vast, conspicuous and dreary, warning all to meddle not with Satan or his ways.

THE SMOTHERED PIPER OF THE WEST CLIFFS

In days gone by there were no houses on the cliffs between the castle and the St Andrews Aquarium, just grassland used for grazing sheep and cattle and much used by local children as a playground. Slightly to the west of Butts Wynd, on the face of the cliffs, was the entrance to a cold dark cave, a cave much feared by locals. It had many names over the years including the 'Jingling Cave', 'John's Coal Hole' and 'The Piper's Cave'. The opening was said to be very small but once inside a grown man would be able to pass down a passageway into a chamber with further passages branching off. Though many locals knew of the cave, few ventured inside and none ever ventured beyond the dark, creepy chamber with its Latin Cross carved into the wall.

In a small two-roomed cottage in Argyle Street lived an old woman, Auld Maggie Laing. She lived in one room and her son, Wullie, his wife and new bairn lived in the other. He was a bit of a daredevil and well known as a good piper; in fact it's said he was the best in Fife, a piper who would have pleased even Maggie Lauder. He was often to be seen, and heard, in the pubs and alehouses of the town making the rafters ring with his music. He was also very interested in the story of the West Cliff Cave. One night, they say it was the night of the Lammas Fair, he found himself in the Castle Tavern with some friends. Maybe he'd had one too many drams, but he found himself taking a bet that on the next New Year's night he would investigate the cave and play the pipes up as far as he could go. In the next few months his mother, his wife and many of his friends tried to dissuade him from doing such a stupid thing. He was determined though, after all, a bet was a bet. So, on a dark New Year's Eve he entered the cave, pipes playing merrily and loudly, watched by a group of friends. They were able to follow the sound of the pipes until the sound passed beneath Market Street, when it stopped, suddenly. Wullie and his pipes were never seen again. Somewhere, beneath the town, lies the whitened bones of the piper lad, his famous pipes still beside him.

Many attempts were made to find him, but no one ever did. Not even the bravest of his friends would dare go beyond the entrance of that foul, dark passage. His mother and his wife were overcome with grief, and the young wife used to spend hours sitting at the mouth of the cave, waiting for her Wullie to return. Finally, her mind gave way and she began wandering down to the cave at all hours of the day and night and in all weathers. The following New Year's Eve she left the little cottage in Argyle Street and, wrapping herself in her shawl, she turned to the old woman and said, 'Tak care o' the bairn. I'm awa tae my Wullie.' Morning came but she never returned home.

She had indeed gone to her lost Wullie. For years afterwards the small crouching figure of a woman, dim and shadowy, could be seen on moonlit nights perched on a rock by the cave. Wild shrieks and sounds of pipe music were constantly heard coming from the same entrance. And, much later, when the houses were built and the entrance covered over, Piper Wullie could still be seen, walking 'where no mortal should be able to walk' where the edge of the old cliffs used to be, his presence heralded by an icy blast.

THE MAIDEN CASTLE

Between West Lomond and Bishop Hill a huge regular green mound lies. It is said that a Caledonian Chief is laid to rest there with his betrothed, who died with him in battle.

Aleph, a brave fighter who conquered all he fought and who brought many riches to his family and followers, was betrothed to a young maiden who worshipped him, the bonniest lassie in the land. The day of the wedding dawned but not in peace. The war cry of a hostile band rang out, thirsting to avenge their shattered honour. A fierce battle followed. Blue-eyed Aleph was at the head, tawny locks blowing, weapons flashing, inspiring his followers. The battle rolled outside the camp, close to the earthen ramparts from where the women watched, amongst who was Unena, Aleph's beloved. She watched her hero proudly then, seized with terror, she saw him fall and watched as the seething mass hacked his fallen body. She didn't cry out but sprang into their midst. Too late Aleph's followers noticed, and, unable to shield her, all they could do was gather round the bodies of the fallen pair. Aleph's followers won the battle and carried the pair to a glade where they buried them with ceremonial rite. They piled on them the Chieftain's arms and weapons and covered them with a mantle of the rarest fur to be found in Fife. And over them was built a mound which took seven days to complete. The chief's gold and all his treasures were deposited in the mound secretly by the high priest.

'Twas done at midnight when the silver moon shone at her full. The silent moon alone the spot did mark and kept the secret, keeps it still.'

Thus the maiden castle was built. It is said that the bonniest pair of youthful lovers in the Kingdom may find the treasure if they wander, hand-in-hand, seven times around the tomb when the moon is at its fullest. Then the earth shall give up the hidden treasure.

Tales of Kemback

Almost from its beginning the old house of Kemback was a quiet family residence, far off the beaten track, where its lairds and their families spent peaceful as well as stormy days. The house is screened from the road by dense woodland and probably few of the many visitors passing through Dura Den every summer ever see it. It's the stormy times that provide the interesting stories told round local firesides to anyone who cared to listen.

In 1655, one laird was known to have been found drowned at the side of the Eden at a place called the Haugh. The previous day he had been drinking ale and strong spirits at the house of a friend in Cupar along with other lairds, including the Laird of Dairsie. The kirk session of Cupar looked into it but could do nothing since the folk involved lived outside the parish. They did find out, however, that he had arrived at his friend's house between seven and eight and had remained there for eight hours. It was assumed that he had been on his way home full of drink when he fell in the river at the Haugh and was drowned. However, the unofficial story told amongst the locals was one of an argument between the friends over money, resulting in a fight and subsequent drowning.

In another tale it is said that one laird suffered persecution for his beliefs. He had to leave the house and hide in a cave, still there today high on the rocks above Dura Den. It was winter and his wife carried food to him daily, tying her shoes on back to front so to confuse anyone who tried to follow her.

Eventually she was found out and captured. Refusing to betray her husband, she was hanged over Dairsie Bridge and beheaded. Popular tradition has it that she is the White Lady of Kemback, whose headless effigy in stone lies in a wood near the house and after whom a room in the mansion was long-named the White Lady's Room. Many locals claim to have seen a headless White Lady wandering the pathway between the house and the cave in the cliff on dark winter's evenings.

A later laird had in his younger day been in Prince Charles' army and had fought at Culloden. In the battle he was seriously wounded. The story goes that he took refuge in a house on the borders of Culloden Moor. When the government soldiers came to search for fugitives the farmer's wife hid him in a meal chest and he lay there staunching his wounds with meal. He made his way back but had another narrow escape on the way, having been given refuge in another house. Leaping from a second-storey window he ran past the church and the minister's wife hid him under a pile of sticks. He made it home only to find soldiers waiting for him so fled once more, this time on horseback. Making his way through the trees, he reached a large boulder high above the river. It is said that he and his horse leapt from the boulder into the water and again escaped, forever leaving a hoof print on that boulder know to this day as 'Charlie's Stane'. This time he managed to make his way to Guardbridge, where he boarded a French smuggler and was taken to France. He lived there for many years before making his peace with the government and retiring to Kemback.

The grounds of the house are well wooded and have several old trees, one of which is associated with a family story. At the gate there stood a lime tree. It is said that when he was courting his future wife, one laird pulled a branch from a lime tree growing in the grounds of her family home to use as a staff or crop as his horse was lazy. On returning home to Kemback he stuck the branch into the ground by the gate. It grew and budded and for many years it was known as the Staff Tree.

There is also a tradition that a subterranean passage runs from Kemback House to Dairsie Castle, underneath the river. A very old woman in the early 1900s told the story that her grandmother told her that when alterations were being made to the house the mouth of the passage was discovered. A travelling piper was persuaded to enter the passage, playing his pipes to see which direction it went in. The piping was heard below ground as far as the river and then it stopped. The piper never returned and after what they thought was a reasonable passage of time, the people built up the mouth of the hole. There's a hollow in the wall but whether that's part of the passage or not is unknown.

Another story connected with the house is the story of Heiland Jenny. It is said that Jenny, having fallen in love with a soldier, followed him to Fife only to be cast aside. She found a job as a housemaid in Kemback House, where she worked for many years. Eventually she moved to a little house in the village at the bottom of the steep steps that led from Kemback to Blebocraigs. Here it is said she brewed her own ale and set up an illicit still in the wash-house, using the clear spring water that flowed there. This she distributed to weary travellers who often paused at the bottom of the steps. Most of the travellers welcomed the cool draught but heaven help any that Jenny didn't like the look of or any who offended her because she also knew a great deal about herbs and something might just be added to the drink, causing upset before they reached their destination.

DOWN THE DRAIN

Often when a castle or cottage has become just a memory, an oak, an ash or a chestnut tree planted beside it survives to remind us what once was there. So it is where the mansion of Balhouffie stood. A great tree marked the spot where a deep drain to the burn also remained, and a tale is told of two adventurous farmhands determined to explore what was to them a mysterious subterranean passage. No doubt they had listened around the fireside to stories and legends of enchanted caves, lost pipers and figures seated in chairs of gold in halls hidden from the world above.

Now the farmer happened to overhear the lads scheming and plotting and noted the time after work they planned their adventure to start. He decided to get there before them so he slipped away to the entrance before the appointed time. Lighting his lamp, he crawled well into the depths, far enough to be out of sight of anyone who chose to enter. The lads eventually appeared with their own light. The adventure looked to them less appealing now that the night was closing in and mysterious voices seemed to mingle with the rush of the burn. Yet they lacked the courage to abandon, neither wanting to lose face before the other. With anxious but determined faces they crept in one after the other, the bolder first. They had penetrated just a few yards when they heard a sound that froze their blood and halted their progress. It was as if a groan of terrible anguish had been forced from tortured lips. This was followed by the clanking of chains. The boys were convinced that they were approaching some long-forgotten dungeon haunted by the spirits of unhappy prisoners who had pined in solitude and darkness till death had at last brought release. Fearing what they might be about to encounter they turned and ran. The story they told grew in the retelling and more and more gloomy tales abounded until the old house and its environs were left to silence and nature.

8

TALES OF THE COAST

Fife certainly has plenty of coastline. Bounded to the north by the River Tay and to the south by the River Forth and to the east by the North Sea, it is almost surrounded by water, so it is no wonder that the sea features often in these folk tales.

KING OF THE SMUGGLERS

One January night a large consignment of brandy was run ashore at the foot of Willie Gray's Dyke between Cellardyke and Caiplie, from where it was transported the few hundred yards to Baillie Andrew Waddell's store in Cellardyke. Later, under the cover of darkness, it was moved again, this time to James Wilson's tavern in Anstruther, known locally as the Smugglers Howff. Here the story might have ended because customs officers were lying in wait and the whole lot was seized.

Delighted at their good luck, the excise men made preparations to sell the contraband goods by public roup, as was the custom. For Andrew Wilson, King of the Smugglers, this was the last straw. A native of Dysart, he was a baker to trade but his more adventurous nocturnal activities had made him a hero up and down the Fife coast. Lately, however, the customs men had seemed to know his every move and this latest setback would leave him a ruined man.

But he was not beaten yet. A few days later he was in Edinburgh recruiting a pair of accomplices to help him carry out a daring plan to 'recover his own'. A day later the three men crossed the Forth to Kinghorn, hired horses and, accompanied by the horse owner's son, made their separate ways to Anstruther. By nightfall they had all stabled their horses at James Wilson's tavern. But they were too late. The brandy had been sold and the excise men were on their way back to Kirkcaldy with the money. But still all was not lost because the excise men were planning to spend the night at Widow Fowler's inn in Pittenweem's Marygate. There were inns and taverns aplenty in Anstruther itself but all were notorious haunts of smugglers. This inn belonging to Mrs Fowler, an excise man's widow, seemed a better bet for a good night's sleep. Later that night, the three desperados attacked the little tavern in Pittenweem, so terrifying the customs men that they leapt out of their second-storey window, leaving behind the money. While two of them hid in a field the third ran barefoot and in his shirt tails to Anstruther to alert the military. The villains were caught red-handed with the money and taken to Edinburgh to stand trial. One was let off with a prison sentence but Wilson and the other man were condemned to be hanged in the Grassmarket. An escape attempt failed when, after procuring a saw and sawing through the bars of the cell, Wilson, the bigger of the two, insisted on going first and got stuck. Feeling guilty, Wilson made one last attempt to help his young companion escape. The Sunday before the hanging the condemned men were taken to the Tollbooth Kirk for their last service. At the end, as the congregation rose, Wilson grabbed the two guards and bit one on the shoulder, shouting, 'Run, George, run!' George ran and got away but Wilson was hanged the next day.

The Crail Skate

Skate can grow to immense sizes, sometimes weighing more than the average man, but none was more remarkable than the one landed by a local Crail fisherman. When first landed the fish just lay on the ground quietly, but when the fishmonger began to prepare it for market it leapt from the table, bit and wounded several bystanders, and the pieces they had already cut off began to leap about and escape into the street. Everyone was not only amazed but terrified too, so they ran away. One Kirk elder though was a bit braver and he dared to return, followed cautiously by the others. Eventually they collected all the bits but when they were all gathered together the fish seemed to come to life again and begin leaping about. So a coffin was made, a good decent coffin, and the creature was buried, not in the churchyard but as near the churchyard wall as possible. Its enormous size was the subject of much speculation and the common belief was that the fish must have fed on some human remains at the bottom of the sea and with the flesh had taken on some human characteristics. The loss of the creature caused much disappointment though because skate was highly sought after as an aphrodisiac. The fertility of fishermen was attributed to the eating of dried skate or 'the merry meat', while the liquid it was cooked in, skate broth or Bree, was supposed to awaken sexual urges. Childless women were often told, 'Awa and sup skate Bree,' and dried skate was given as a wedding present to ensure a large family.

CAULD IRON

In days gone by the folk of St Monans were divided into two groups. Those who stayed in the Nethertown by the shore were fisherfolk, taking a living from the sea. Those who stayed in the Uppertown by the windmill were farmers who took their living from the land. Now the fisherfolk from the Nethertown had a particular hatred of pigs. They saw them as symbols of evil. So much so that not one was kept amongst them. In fact, if one of them happened to even see a pig accidentally they would stop what they were doing and run from it as from a lion, and any job they were about to do, including setting out to sea, would be abandoned until the tide had ebbed and flowed and the spell broken. However, pigs were kept by the farmers in the Uppertown from where they frequently escaped, causing much annoyance and disruption. Eventually the decision was made by the Nethertown folk to destroy not the swine, for they daren't hurt them, but those who bred them. Armed with boathooks they ascended the hill in a formidable procession. But they were spotted by the Uppertown folk, who immediately set loose the pigs. Their grunts and squeals chilled the blood of the most heroic of the fishermen and they turned and ran back down the hill faster than ever, hiding until the tide had ebbed and flowed and the spell was broken. But this state of affairs couldn't go on. The Uppertown folk approached the Lord of the Manor, asking him to intercede with his Nethertown tenants and persuade them that their complaint against the swine was wholly imaginary. But they did so in vain: the fisherfolk could cite many an example of suffering and disaster directly linked to someone having looked on one of the beasts. So the feudal baron had no alternative but to decree the extermination of all pigs from the neighbourhood and tradition has it that no pig existed around St Monans for nearly a century, until they were reintroduced by Sir William Sandilands.

Now, it was customary to transport the pigs 'in a poke', but on one occasion a pig escaped, having gnawed a hole in the sack, and ran off towards Nethertown, closely pursued by its owner. A fisherman with his nets happened to be on the road at that very moment and, seeing the pig, turned and ran home as fast as he could, but he was in such a panic he fell from the end of the pier. As the pig sped through the town many folk saw it and followed it as if under its spell. When it got to the kirk gate someone grabbed the iron latch and called out three times the name St Monan and the spell was broken. From then on the touching of 'Cauld Iron' was thought enough to dissolve the spell.

But not everyone knew of the fisherfolk's aversion to pigs. A young minister, new to the parish, found himself with a full kirk on his first Sunday, the parishioners having been drawn there by curiosity. Unfortunately, he chose the story of the Prodigal Son as the basis of his sermon, thus quashing any hope of ever being popular in the parish because he was obliged to use the words, 'And he sent him into the fields to feed the swine.'

Immediately 'Cauld Iron!' in a strong whisper burst forth from a hundred mouths, accompanied by a desperate stretching

of necks, arms and eyes to find the nearest nail head on which
to place their finger. The minister paused and stared in astonishment, completely unable to work out what was going on.
Eventually he decided that this might be their way of saying
'amen' so he carried on, beginning where he had left off, 'Well,
to feed the swine.'

At this the disorder was renewed. 'Cauld Iron!' rang out, not
in a whisper this time but at such volume that it rebounded
from every nook and cranny of the kirk. The minister again
stopped, petrified, this time fearing that perhaps the kirk was
about to fall down around them, causing the sudden confusion
and panic. Seeing no apparent danger though, he carried on a
little farther, pronouncing, 'The husks that the swine did eat.'

Unable to stand a third shock to their feelings the congregation, in one movement, stood, bolted from the pews and
jumped from the galleries, and with torn clothes and shattered
shins the kirk was in an instant emptied of the whole seafaring
population and many of their descendants never see more than
the outside of the kirk to this day.

THE ABBEY BELLS

It is said that there was once an abbey on a small rocky island off
the coast of Fife inhabited by very hardworking, pious monks.
It was well hidden amongst the cliffs and only the ringing of
its bells signalled where it was. The abbot and monks who
lived there had many valuable treasures to look after. Paintings,
statues, tapestries, golden cups and crosses, but they all agreed
that their most precious treasures were the abbey bells. In the
bell tower they had bells that could peal out the most glorious
sound you could ever imagine. And they were made of solid
gold. One of the monks, Brother John, was particularly fond

of the bells. He was new to the abbey and he was young and strong so every day he would be found up in the tower ringing the bells. He would pull the ropes and watch them swing back and forth. But it was the sound they made that he loved most of all.

The only other thing he loved, almost as much as ringing the bells, was sleeping. It took a great deal of effort to wake him.

The abbey was close to the sea, so close that at night the monks would fall asleep to the lapping of the waves. Sometimes they would see ships and occasionally someone would row ashore to visit them. That way they kept up to date with what was happening in the world. When pirates were seen in the area, putting ashore to rob the lonely crofts, the monks were always amongst the first to hear about it.

One summer morning a local fisherman came to tell them pirates were about and that they should keep out of sight and keep quiet. If the pirates heard about them and their treasures they would be in trouble. The monks agreed to keep out of sight. They had a cave nearby where they could hide with their treasure if they needed to. That was all they did though and life went on as before.

About a week later, early in the morning, the monk who was on lookout saw a strange ship drop anchor in the bay. He could just make out a black flag fluttering from the mast … it was the Jolly Roger – pirates! He could see them getting their boats ready to come ashore. Not daring to make too much noise in case the pirates heard, the monk ran amongst the brothers, telling them what he had seen. Without making a fuss they decided to hide themselves and the treasure. They gathered their precious things and left by the back door, heading for their secret cave. All except one monk that is.

Brother John didn't leave with them because he was still sleeping. He slept and he snored until even he had slept enough. Then he yawned, rubbed his eyes and sat up.

'Goodness,' he thought as he looked around the empty dormitory. 'They must have let me have a long lie in. I wonder why? Still, I'm awake now … time to ring the bells.' He stumbled sleepily over to the bell tower and let himself in.

Meanwhile, the pirates had come ashore, armed to the teeth, to find out if there was anything worth stealing. The abbey was quite well hidden and they had missed it as they scouted around. They had just decided to return to the ship when the bells began to ring.

'Aha! So there is something here!' said the pirate captain.

Meanwhile, Brother John was enjoying himself ringing the bells but he stopped short when the door flew open and the pirates burst in. What an evil-looking bunch they were. They tied him up and barged around the place looking for treasure, but the abbey was empty, there was nothing that interested them.

'The only valuable things I can see are the bells,' said the pirate captain. 'At least we can take them. Look lively you lot. Get them on board and let's get out of here.' It was hard work taking down the bells and carrying them to the shore and then rowing them back to the ship. But at last they succeeded and got them stowed below decks. The pirates even forgot about Brother John, who was still tied up and powerless to stop them taking the bells.

Once the pirates were gone, the other monks came out of hiding and found him alone in the bell tower.

'The pirates have stolen the bells,' he called. 'What are we to do?'

'Never mind,' said the abbot, 'those bells won't do the pirates any good on land or water. And we can always get new bells.'

The abbot was right. As soon as the pirates had hoisted the sails and weighed anchor, the bells started rolling about in the hold. They rolled with the pitching of the sea and as they did they rang out as if they were laughing at the pirates. Then, one by one, they crashed through the side of the ship and disappeared beneath the waves. Water poured in through the holes and the pirates had to lower their boats again and row for their lives.

Back at the abbey, the abbot ordered new bells. When they arrived, Brother John was the first to be allowed to ring them. As for the old bells, they settled down on the seabed and to this day, as the currents flow around them, there are times when you can hear them if you listen very carefully.

THE SEVEN YOUNG CASTAWAYS

The year was 1710. Seven young boys at school in St Andrews, the oldest just fifteen years, got hold of a boat with a pair of oars in it, skipped school and set off for an adventure. It wasn't the first time they'd set sail around the bay, having taken short trips along the east sands as far as the Maiden Stone and Kinkell Cave, even venturing as far as Kinkell Ness. Sometimes they went the other way around the castle, but always, like chickens coming home to roost, they had found their way back again, moored their boat, clambered up the brae and home again, with their parents none the wiser nor worse for their short sea voyage.

But this particular day, the 19th of August, was a beautiful day. The sun shining, the sea clear and calm, the gulls wheeling and diving above them, the young lads decided to venture further afield. The wind was from the south west, causing just the gentlest of swells on the water, and cooling the sweating brows of the young rowers.

Suddenly a few 'goats' hairs' in the sky above and a few 'cats' paws' on the water gave warning of something stronger coming and that it was time to turn back. But in their anxiety to return the old proverb 'Mair haste, waur speed' was proven true because they either broke the rollocks or lost an oar, so, like a fly in treacle or a duck swimming with one leg, they could make no headway whatever, but drifted helplessly out to sea.

There was no lifeboat in those days, in fact there was very little traffic from the harbour at all. No one came to their rescue; no one even noticed them. For six whole days and nights they were tossed around, drifting helplessly in the bay. There were no tempting provisions of a modern-day picnic party either. They had neither water nor bread aboard; how they managed we don't know, perhaps collecting rainwater and grabbing the occasional curious fish swimming by.

You can imagine the state of these poor boys, the elements against them, as well as fear, hunger, thirst, anxiety and exhaustion each taking its toll.

At last on the sixth day they were washed ashore at the base of a high rock known as 'High Heugh', about fifty miles from St Andrews, near Aberdeen. They were so worn out from

hunger, thirst and lack of sleep that they could hardly crawl from the boat, never mind climb the cliff. But two of the strongest did, with great endeavour, manage to climb up to the top and were found by a kindly old fisherman named Shepherd, who lived nearby. With great care and gentleness he was able to get the boys to his home, where he did everything to restore them to health, including getting medical aid from Aberdeen. Despite this, two of the boys died. The other five though were nursed back to health and restored to their anxious parents.

The recovery of the oldest was greatly enhanced by the special care he received from a young blue-eyed lass, the same age as the lad and granddaughter of the kind fisherman.

The father of this young man, whose name was Bruce, a citizen of Edinburgh, was so grateful for the care and attention his son had received from the fisherman and his granddaughter, that he gave them a present of a silver plate, engraved with a picture showing the young boys landing amongst the rocks.

The Sinking of *The Fox*

The year was 1865, April market day in St Andrews. William Thomson, known locally as 'Billy the Boy', was out bringing in his creels.

Billy Thomson was in his sixties, and got his nickname from his habit of taking too much grog, or 'wetting both his eyes' too often and swaggering about the Lady Head, bareheaded and often with nothing more on than his drawers, squaring with his fists, bouncing and running after the young lads, swearing by the most dreadful oaths that he was 'Billy the Boy' and he would do for the 'wracks' as he called them, more in jest than in anger.

With him were two twenty year olds, Henry Waters and Jamie Wilson. Davie Gardner, another member of the crew, didn't sail with them that day because he'd been asked to pilot a schooner.

They had taken their yawl, *The Fox*, out into the bay for some fishing and to collect in their creels. They were heading for home, Billy steering, the others tidying up their lines, when a sudden squall struck the boat about a mile north-east of the pier head. She filled and sank quickly because she was laden with a good catch

No one saw her sink, but a brother of Henry Waters was standing on the pier waiting for her to come in. He turned his back for a minute and when he looked seaward again he couldn't see her. Alarmed, he ran up the Kirkhill, but still he couldn't see her so he ran down again, got another man, unmoored his own boat and set out as fast as he could.

All they saw was the top of Billy's head and the ends of two bladders, which he'd grabbed in his death grip, sticking above the water. Billy was a heavy man so it was with great difficulty they hauled him aboard. It was said there was life still in him but onshore, though Dr Adamson was called immediately, he was declared dead. The next day the bodies of the other two were dragged up within ten yards of where she sank. Her creels, ballast, fish and lines were still aboard when the yawl herself was hauled up, the very oars still in place.

The loss of these three lives caused a great sensation in the town and when the other two bodies and the boat were brought into the harbour, a great crowd lined the pier.

The Fox went once again to sea, once only, sent by her new owner, Jack Waters, who was often described as a queer, industrious fisherman. Driven, like a deserter out of a regiment, out of the harbour, with several holes smashed through her bottom, so angry at his brother's death, he vowed, 'She'll niver droon anither.'

But as if to prove that 'the best laid schemes gang aft agley' she might have done so, because there being a strong south-westerly wind and not wanting to sink, *The Fox* floated over and went ashore on Kinshaldy beach.

JOHN HONEY

The morning of the 5th of January 1800 was bitterly cold. The blinding sleet driving before the biting wind forced all who could to stay indoors listening to the crashing breakers and the howl of the wind as it swept over St Andrews Bay. Unless forced by duty or business, none dared to face the storm along the Scores or at the harbour. On this particular day a party of gentlemen from the coast happened to be sitting cosily in the parlour of the old Black Bull Inn, the chief inn of the city then, near the east end of South Street, possibly drinking some smuggled whisky from Glenfarg.

Suddenly the sound of running feet was heard outside and the cry of 'Ship ashore! Ship ashore!' roused them to action because such a cry was an advertisement of an exciting entertainment which always drew a large audience, especially if there was the prospect of someone being drowned before their eyes. In a minute the room was empty. Hats and coats grabbed from their pegs they rushed to the door. There was no need to ask which way to run for the thrilling cry of 'Ship ashore!' had already roused the townsfolk. Shoemakers in their black aprons, bakers in their white aprons and even whiter faces, students in their red cloaks, schoolboys, sailors and the general public with anxious faces rushed eastwards along South Street, Market Street and North Street in the direction of the harbour to the Kirk Hill, which overlooked the piers and the bay in the direction of the Kinkell Braes. One glance was enough to see through the sleet a ship grounded amidst the surf at the East Sands.

On hurrying down to the East Bents, where a crowd was already gathered, a heartrending and thrilling sight was to be seen. There, quite close to the shore, was the sloop *Janet* almost buried amidst the breakers, which smashed against her and over her with irresistible force, shrouding her in surf and driving sleet. Through all this, those on shore could occasionally glimpse the crew clinging with despair to the rigging, which lay within 300 yards of where they stood. Amidst the dull roar could be heard the murmured, 'What can be done? How can we save them?' No one knew. There were many brave and daring men in the crowd but none could, nor none dared face the raging sea to rescue the ill-fated seamen.

Suddenly a ripple of applause ran through the excited throng. 'He will go! He has offered!' resounded from a knot of students, one of them shouting, 'Bring me a rope! I will try and save them!'

'There, pressing forward, was a stalwart young student, John Honey, tearing off his clothes, heedless of the onlookers, preparing to battle with the angry sea. Tying the rope around his waist, a knife between his teeth, he dashed into the surf and struck out, swimming towards the wreck. He made little headway, for each breaking wave seemed to hurl him back. His progress was slow and success so doubtful that at last, when almost at the wreck, the half despairing wail arose, 'He will never reach the sloop! Let's save him! He will be drowned! Pull him back!' And this well-meant design was put into action. The slack of the rope was hauled in, but it broke and his anxious friends pulled in not John Honey but a now useless coil of rope. He had cut it to prevent his friends stopping his rescue attempt. His eye was on the drowning men when he severed his connection with the shore. Then, with renewed strength and skill, he made his way to the side of the ship, clambered up and stood on the deck of the stranded sloop. The crowd gasped when they saw him: 'He's made it!' they cried. He was seen to give a word of encouragement to the crew before fastening the end of the other rope to the ship. Then he waited his chance, poised on the edge before he sprang into the seething waves to be hurled like a cork back to the shore and his waiting friends. Amid the buzz of welcome and much handshaking he managed to convey that he needed them to hold the other end of the rope. But alas, four days of cold and sleepless anxiety had robbed the crew of the power to use the slender bridge now firmly attached to both wreck and shore. Must they now perish despite the effort made by Honey? Not yet! Again Honey dashed into the waves and, availing himself of the rope bridge, he managed to reach again the now rapidly breaking-up sloop to stand once more on the deck. Grabbing the nearest seaman, he returned to shore, this time not alone. Without a word he staggered ashore with his almost senseless burden and then once again rushed back through the surf to the stranded sloop. This heroic work he repeated again and again until the captain and three of the crew were returned to shore. Only the slight form of a boy could now be seen clinging to the wreck, much higher up than the others had been. Honey was so exhausted that it seemed the youngest of the crew would be lost, for none in the crowd seemed able to fill the gap. The boy shrieked in terror and on hearing this Honey leapt to his feet, seized the rope and dashed once more into the waves, and, although not as quickly as before, reached the now shattered wreck. With great difficulty he clambered aboard, climbed up the shredded sails and rested a few seconds by the poor helpless lad. The crash of the mast spurred him on to descend to the deck and he was seen slowly sinking over the side, clutching the swaying rope bridge as he attempted to reach the shore.

'There is only one head visible!' 'The boy has been swept away!' 'He has let go of the rope!' 'He is lost!' several voices exclaimed at once. But no! Honey, with what seemed like superhuman strength, was able to grab the boy and place the rope in his hand only to lose him again. Once more Honey dived into the seething waves and seized the boy in his arms as the next breaker picked them up and flung them to shore as if in pity. The boy and his equally exhausted rescuer lay senseless and almost lifeless on the wet sand. The crowd, who had up till now watched in stillness, began to cheer.

But although the crew were all safely cared for in the old Black Bull Inn and as far as is known completely recovered from their ordeal, John Honey didn't fare so well. Saving the lives of others cost him his own. The soaking he got that night left him with a weak chest and he died a few years later at the age of thirty-two.

PIRATES COME TO KIRKCALDY

Kirkcaldy had no more thrilling happening in its long history than the impressive account of the manner in which the town and the whole of the Firth of Forth was saved from Paul Jones, the American privateer, and his fleet.

It was the 17th of September 1778. Jones and his ships had been heading for Leith when they found themselves driven by the wind towards the Fife coast. On board one of the ships happened to be a man from Pittenweem named Taylor, who had left the town on being charged with the maintenance of a natural child. He assured the captain that they would be safe in this port but the wind had other ideas and the ships drifted towards Kirkcaldy. At the sight of the ships bearing down on them, the ballies and the magistrates and all the terrified residents thronged to the beach, bringing every means of resistance they possessed. A few pistols and cutlasses, two dozen ancient and primitive firelocks, iron bars, clubs, even scythes were pressed into what was seen to be almost hopeless service.

Nearer and nearer drew the pirate ships, beating up the Firth against a strong head wind. The watchers on the shore had lost all hope when a tall grave-looking man came upon the scene. It was the minister, Mr Shirra.

'The Lord reigneth!' he cried. 'He'll stop the pirates with the guns of heaven; my friends, let us pray!'

The whole crowd knelt down on the sand and the good man with great earnestness entreated God to preserve them. Within five minutes the wind suddenly veered round two or three points to the west and began to blow strongly straight down the Forth. Before Mr Shirra's prayer could change from one of supplication to one of thanksgiving the pirates were almost out of sight and Kirkcaldy was safe once more.

The Buccaneers of Buckhaven

In days gone by the people of Buckhaven kept themselves very much to themselves and were regarded as outsiders by other Fife folk and to be of foreign origin descended either from the crew of a Dutch ship wrecked on the coast or, more commonly, from a gang of Dutch buccaneers who took shelter on the Fife coast.

The buccaneers had found themselves in Berwick-upon-Tweed, having been pursued all around the coast by the English authorities. There were many of them and soon they began to fight amongst themselves. After a fierce battle the winning group, fearing the English law, headed northwards. They landed in Fife, sought and got permission from the Earl of Wemyss to settle where they came ashore and chose the little 'hyne' or haven to build their dwellings. They named it Buckhaven, partly after the vast amount of buckie shells they found there and partly on account of the battle which they had had with their neighbours in Berwick, which had brought them to Fife in the first place, because in those days the buccaneers would say 'bucking' when they meant fighting. They spoke their own tongue for many a year and continued to dress as they had always done, until the weather and work forced them to conform to Fife ways.

As time went by they lost their buccaneering ways and gained the reputation of being a sober, sensible, industrious and honest set of people.

The only part of their past custom which remained was their belief in bogles of all kinds and forms. They believed in ghosts and fairies and witches who sailed over the sea in cockleshells. They believed in the kelpie water spirits who often appeared as horses and made a dreadful roar before a boat was lost at sea. They feared maukins or hares because they believed that witches turned themselves into these creatures. They believed that Willy the Wisp or 'Spunkie' was a fiery devil who led folk to their death, and many a good boat coming to land at night-time would see a light and head for it only to be dashed on the rocks.

They weren't, however, considered to be quite so well mannered and well educated as some Fifers and, except to the folk of Buckhaven themselves, the term 'College of Buckhyne' was a much appreciated and longstanding joke. It used to be said of any young lad who was particularly backward or uncouth, 'he's surely been brought up in the college of Buckhyne'. In fact, it shared with the 'Back Muirs of Gilston' in the lands beyond Norrie's Law, the distinction of being the least 'cultured' locality in Fife.

The 'college' was a two-storeyed house to the east of the old village used to conceal smuggled goods. Duty free gin led to drunken brawls and Maillie, the wife of a sailor, was killed in one of these. Her ghost was believed to haunt the place and anyone who had cause to go that way after dark went by way of the beach rather than pass it.

KING OF THE FISH

Davie didn't like fish. He didn't like the smell of it, he didn't like the feel of it and he didn't like the taste of it, which was unfortunate because the only job he could get at eighteen was working for an old fisherman. Every day they went to sea and the skipper would tip the catch onto the deck and it was Davie's job to cut off the fish heads and take out the guts. Davie hated that bit of the work. One beautiful day the skipper dumped a mackerel on the deck for gutting. Davie admired the beautiful colours and the bright eye of the fish. When he felt it wriggling in his fingers he couldn't bring himself to kill it. So he hid it behind his back and when the skipper wasn't looking he slipped it back over the side of the boat into the sea. He gave it back its life.

But the skipper had seen and there was a terrible argument.

'Do you think I go to sea every day getting soaked to the skin and only scraping a living from the fish for you to throw them back?' he shouted at the boy.

Davie took a break and stood before the mast whistling. Now you never should whistle on a fishing boat for if you do you're either whistling up the Devil or whistling up the wind. This made the skipper even more furious. In fact, he sacked him on the spot, telling him that he must leave the boat as soon as they reached harbour and never set foot on it again.

Davie was half glad and half sad. He was half glad because he hated the job anyway but he was half sad because he knew he would have to go home and tell his wife he was out of work again.

He left the boat and climbed the ladder onto the quay, his eyes filling with tears and the corners of his mouth turned down.

On his way home Davie realised he had company. There was a strange man walking beside him, leading a black and white cow. If Davie had looked carefully he would have noticed two little horns on top of the stranger's head and a red tail sticking out of the back of his trousers. Of course it was Auld Nick, the Devil himself. He asked why Davie looked so sad and Davie told him about losing his job and that he was going to have to go home and tell his wife.

The Devil told Davie that if he had the black and white cow he wouldn't be out of work because the cow gave the richest and creamiest milk there ever was. Davie and his wife could make butter, cheese and ice-cream and even open a wee tearoom like they always dreamed of. He said Davie could borrow the cow for three years. But, when he came back to collect it, he would ask Davie three questions. If Davie couldn't answer them he would be thrown over the Devil's shoulder and carried away to burn in Hell.

To Davie three years was a long time off and at eighteen he thought himself invincible. He shook hands with the Devil and a bargain was struck. The Devil handed Davie the rope which was tied round the cow's neck and they headed for home. As the Devil did a somersault and disappeared down a crack in the earth, Davie thought he would never set eyes on him again.

Davie's wife was looking out the window watching for him to come home. When she saw him walking up the lane leading a black and white cow she was surprised. Davie had brought home friends before, he'd brought home fish before, but he'd never before brought home a cow.

She rushed out to meet him, asking what was going on. Proudly, Davie told her that the cow gave the richest and creamiest milk there ever was and they were going to open a tearoom like they'd always wanted as he had given up the fishing.

Davie and his wife did open the tearoom and its fame soon spread up and down the coast and they did very well and Davie forgot all about the stranger and the bargain he had struck. But three years to the day Davie was in the tearoom mopping the floor with only one customer, a stranger, left sitting in the corner. Suddenly there was a flash of blue light and there was Auld Nick himself. He had polished his skin up bright red and sharpened his hooves and his tail specially. He looked menacingly at Davie, telling him he had come to collect the cow, but even worse he had three questions to answer and if Davie couldn't answer them he would be off for a tour of Hell.

He asked if Davie was ready, but before Davie could answer, the stranger sitting in the corner of the tearoom answered that Davie was ready and that the Devil had just asked the first question.

The Devil was a bit annoyed at this and asked the stranger to mind his own business. The stranger said he wouldn't and he had just asked the second question. Furious, the Devil asked who this interfering stranger was. The stranger replied that he was the King of the Fish. Three years ago Davie had thrown him back over the side of the fishing boat and saved his life. Now he had come to repay Davie for his kindness. And that, he said, was the third question.

The Devil realised he'd been outwitted and in a tantrum stamped his hoof on the ground, making a hoof print in the concrete, and stormed out of the tearoom. He was in such a sulk that he even forgot to take the cow.

As far as I know Davie and his wife are still there, so if you're ever in a tearoom in Fife have a good look on the floor to see if you can spot a hoof print. If you do, you just might be in Davie's tearoom.

9

WITCHES AND WIZARDS

In Fife, plenty of people believed in witches, wizards and fairies. It wasn't a crime to believe in them or in fact witchcraft, but it was a crime to be a witch and many folk, both high-born and peasant, also believed it was a crime to consort with 'The Queen of Elfhame – the Fairy Queen of Elvenhame,' and her band of fairies. There was a longstanding acceptance of the malign supernatural powers of the fairies. Those spiteful creatures were euphemistically and somewhat contradictorily known as the 'Gude Neighbours' and were seen to be just as much in league with the Devil as the witches and wizards, the connection between black magic and fairies being alluded to at several famous witch trials. Rumours of men and women who had entered into infernal pacts and had become instruments of Satan caused a panic amongst ordinary folk and led to thousands of needless deaths. The stories which grew up around these poor unfortunate women and men would be comical if it wasn't for the tragic endings.

THE BURNING OF MAGGIE MORGAN

The inhabitants of the East Neuk today may know of the visit of King Charles II to the Royal Burgh of Pittenweem in the seventeenth century. Few, however, may realise the weird goings-on which coincided with this historic event. Two local worthies, the minister and the dominie from St Monans, had attended the spectacle in Pittenweem with their respective wives, who happened to be sisters. When it was over, intent of making a day of it, they retired with their spouses to Peter Bizzie's Inn. There, after much drink was taken, they became 'Kings' themselves, elevating the jolly innkeeper to the peerage, and then making him prime minister. When midnight struck, telling them it was time to go, the innkeeper's wife produced the ladies from her private rooms, they too feeling as 'royal' as their menfolk.

Now, by coincidence there was that night a witches meeting on Pittenweem's Witches Loan. Attending was Maggie Morgan from the Overtoun of St Monans. She was there for the purpose of receiving additional powers and to be fully admitted into the black secrets of the sisterhood by inscribing the infernal oath in her own blood. But what had brought Maggie there?

Maggie was a bonnie young farm girl who had caught the eye of a young laird from Elie House. Seduced by his flattery she became pregnant and soon found herself ruined and deserted. Though the villagers felt sorry for her they were powerless to help or question higher authority. After the birth came the inquisition from the minister, whose word on such matters was absolute. He also consulted a well-known clype, who further smeared Maggie's character. Alone, Maggie was brought before the kirk session and, daring to suggest that the child's father was a gentleman, conspicuous by his absence, she was branded a 'harlot and a limmer' by the minister and by the dominie, a known drinking friend of the minister. The other elders followed suit and she was found guilty. Her punishment was to attend the kirk on three successive Sundays dressed in sackcloth; and stand in the vestibule as the congregation arrived chanting 'False tongue that lied'. Then, during the service, she had to stand above the congregation on the penitential stool.

Maggie swore revenge on her seducer and her persecutors but seemed unlikely to achieve her aims against such influential and powerful men. However, one night at the height of a terrible storm she was visited in her cottage by a mysterious woman. The stranger advised her that if she wanted the power to get her own back she should attend the witches coven on the Loan, to be held on the fifth night of the week at ten o'clock. So we find her on the Witches Loan, the very date and time presenting her with the perfect opportunity to strike, not only at the minister but also at his aider and abettor, the dominie.

The night was black, starless and filled with witches, wizards, ghosts and goblins when the two merry couples set their glowing noses towards home. Perhaps such evil would have frightened ordinary mortals unfortified by 'bold John Barleycorn' but the minister always had a word ready for such occasions and the dominie swore that quoting Pythagoras' theorem was enough protection against any devilment.

However, not a quarter of a mile out of town Maggie cast a spell over them. Rooted to the spot, they stood quaking as in a dazzling flash of light they were suddenly confronted by – a white rabbit! As they gazed spellbound, the creature loped around them seven times. This was none other than Maggie bewitching her enemies. By her sorcery they were filled with new energy and laughter and a compulsion to change partners. Their ears filled with merry music, they were irresistibly drawn to the Loan, where they joined in with the revelry, much to the annoyance of the coven. We don't know what unspeakable experiences they suffered at the hands of the witches and warlocks but when it ended they were mysteriously transported back to the very spot where they had first met the rabbit. The women had been stripped of their fine clothes till they nearly breached the laws of decency and the black coats of the men had been replaced by fishermen's guernseys. But Maggie was not done yet and now they saw Auld Nick himself running towards them. Each seizing the other's wife, they took off down the road to St Monans but Auld Nick tapped their heels and up-ended them into a muddy ditch where, tired out by the day's exertions, exhausted by their experiences and befuddled by the drink, they fell asleep.

There they were found in the morning by four ploughmen on their way to work, while grazing nearby was 'Auld Nick' himself, the minister's own cow that had escaped from the byre and strayed off. It was a sorry looking and bedraggled group who retraced their steps to Peter Bizzie's Inn, where they tidied themselves up and sat down to consider the consequences of their escapade. The news would surely reach the ears of the presbytery, and so, fearing excommunication and the loss of their jobs, they decided that the only thing to do was to seek a royal pardon for their actions; after all, the King was still close by and was it not his visit that got them into trouble in the first place.

Tramping through Pittenweem to Anstruther House at the junction of the Crail and St Andrews roads, where the King had spent the night, they asked for an audience. Pathetically they pledged undying loyalty and asked for the King's forgiveness. Charles granted their wish. Thinking that their troubles were now over they happily set off on the road home, but luck was not yet on their side. When they reached the spot where they had met the rabbit and their troubles had started, they found their wives violently arguing with each other. The sisters, now released from the enchantment, had suddenly realised that each had spent the night, albeit innocently, in the arms of the other's husband and were blaming each other for such outrageous conduct. 'Stop!' shouted the dominie, whereupon his wife replied, 'Embrace your mistress, you rakish rooster!' This reply won her a very prompt 'dad on the lug' from her husband, which finished the argument. They all made their separate way home, never to speak to each other again. Tradition has it that the spot was from then on called the 'Daft Hill' and later became 'Taft Hill'.

In the meantime, Maggie, pleased with her triumph and newly found powers, now targeted the real hate of her life, her former lover from Elie House. One morning in June, she saw him with a new lassie on his arm making his way down to St Monans harbour. They were about to set off on a boat trip to the Isle of May. Using her magic, she flew to Pittenweem where she consulted Broon of the Braes, a noted warlock and commander-in-chief of the local coven. He told her to find a secluded spot on the east braes with a good view of the harbour. There she was to float a wooden bowl in a tub of water. When the boat was a good way from the harbour mouth she was to

whirl the bowl around seven times and then cowp it. She flew back to St Monans and prepared her spell, successfully sinking the boat with the words, 'Here, mak yer bridal bed amongst the partans.' The crew swam ashore but the young couple were found drowned the next day at low water.

Maggie's devilish work, however, had not gone unnoticed and the minister, who had suspected her hand in his own affair, worked hard to get evidence for her arrest as a witch. In time she was arrested and charged with being in league with the Devil. Since she was now satisfied that she had had her revenge, Maggie confessed all and pleaded guilty. After a brief trial she was convicted and sentenced to be burned on the Kirk Hill in view of the assembled population. So died Maggie Morgan, the last witch to be burned in St Monans.

THE BEWITCHING TALE OF ALISOUN PEIRSON

High on the Muirs o' Fife, we hear that on moonlit nights the form of Alisoun Peirson can be seen flitting along the banks of the Kenly Burn, from the direction of Boarhills. It is said that three centuries ago she lived in a cottage on the edge of the village and was often found, when the moon was right, collecting plants and herbs along the bank of the burn to use in the making of healing concoctions. Here she was said to meet with a man 'cled in green claithes'. Some said with a certain reluctant pride that this was 'oor ain Scots De'il' but others said it was 'the King o' the Fairies' himself.

But Alisoun's story begins earlier when she was a twelve-year-old child out on Grange Muir. The poor child grew sick and collapsed, probably from catching a chill. Suddenly out of the mists of the Muir, her cousin, Mr William Simpson, appeared as a green man and told her he would help her if she would believe in him. Not waiting for her affirmation he disappeared only to reappear later with a group of fairies in tow. They took Alisoun to a secret glade, whereupon it magically transformed into 'Elfhame' with everyone indulging in the kind of merrymaking and frolics you'd associate with the fairies. During their lengthy association – seven years it is said – the fairy folk were unkind to Alisoun. She was tormented, poked, prodded and beaten, leaving her left side without strength and a blue mark on her skin. Nevertheless, she was initiated into the fairies secrets and shown how to use herbal remedies and make the salves which could kill or cure as desired.

Subsequently, on her return to Boarhills, Alisoun gained a reputation for having healing powers, coming and going to St Andrews to heal folk for many a year. Beyond the locals, who no doubt benefited from her ministrations, Alisoun's reputation eventually brought her into contact with the high and mighty. One of those was said to be Patrick Adamson, the Archbishop of St Andrews, who wasn't popular with the Presbyterians. Alisoun was said to have been introduced to him sometime in 1583, when he was suffering from a serious illness which she is said to have cured. Alisoun's problems seem to have started then as she became an unwitting pawn in a game played out between Patrick and his enemies. She was used as a means of getting at Adamson. By accusing Alisoun of witchcraft they put him in the position of being obliged to show willing in the proceedings against her, forsaking all gratitude he may have felt for her in order to prevent his opponents tarnishing his reputation by alleging an association with a witch.

Alisoun was imprisoned and interrogated by the Kirk Session, and, surprise surprise, they found her guilty. She was handed over to the archbishop to be kept in his castle to await execution. But, according to the story, he did the decent thing and allowed her to 'slip away'.

Alison seems to have avoided attention for a while but five years later she was brought to trial again for the same charge of witchcraft. At this trial the presbytery was shown evidence gathered in Fife by one James Melville. She was convicted on the 28th of May 1588 and after being *wirreit* (strangled) at a stake she was *convicta et combusta* (burned). The same year Adamson was excommunicated and though the sentence was later overturned, the revenue of his see was withdrawn and awarded to Ludovic Stewart, the second Duke of Lennox, and for the rest of his life Patrick Adamson lived in much reduced circumstances supported by charity.

AULD BESSIE BITTEM

Auld Bessie Bittem stayed in Dunfermline town and was looked upon by her neighbours with an uneasy kind of feeling. She was regarded as 'no very canny' and it was thought to be unwise to disagree or meddle with her. Even her big black cat was regarded with suspicion.

One day Bessie appeared at the side of Johnnie's loom and said to him, 'Johnnie, ye'll gang the morn and howk my wee puckle tatties, eh?'

'Deed he'll dae naething o' the kind,' shouted Kirsty, his wife, from the kitchen. 'He has mair need tae dad awa' at his loom an' get his cut oot.'

'He'll maybe no get his cut oot ony the sooner for no howkin' my tatties,' Bessie retorted.

'Maybe ye'd better let me gang,' said Johnnie to his wife.

'Ye'll no gang an that's that,' replied Kirsty.

'Ye'll no let him howk a wee puckle o' tatties for a puir auld body like me! Mind I'm tellin' ye, he'll no be ony the richer for't,' shouted Bessie as she toddled out of the shop, followed by her black cat.

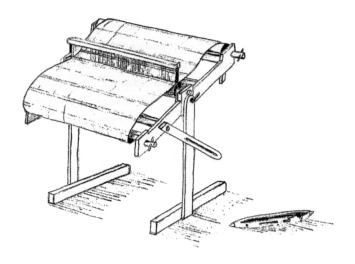

Johnnie had scarcely resumed his work when the shuttle flew out of his hand and landed on the floor. He got down and lifted it up and tried again but with a like result. Again and again it sprang out, giving him the delay and the trouble of going for it. He thought himself bewitched, as if judgement had come on him sooner than he expected. How was he going to break the spell? He had 'neither vervain, nor her dill, that hindered witches of their will, nor Rowan tree or red thread, that put witches to their speed', so he took the shuttle to the kitchen and sat down by the fire with a very long face.

He tried to break the spell by solemnly drawing the shuttle three times through the smoke, dolefully saying as he did so, 'I kent hoo it wad be, I kent hoo it wad be!'

Then he turned to his wife and said, 'O Kirsty! Ye might have hid mair sense than contrar, that auld witch Bessie Bittem!'

THE WIZARD OF BALWEARIE

Sir Michael Scot of Balwearie was an academic who spent a great deal of time studying witchcraft and the black arts abroad. Such was his interest that he got the reputation of being a wizard himself and legend has it that he made many a pact with the Devil and had imps and demons at his beck and call.

One demon he bought in exchange for his shadow. A Fife laird, a wee bit simple perhaps, met Sir Michael out hunting shortly after this transaction. He told Scot his appearance would be greatly improved if he brought his shadow along. No sooner had the laird got out his joke than he felt his sight grow duller. He went home much alarmed but before he got half way there he became completely blind and died falling over a cliff.

On another occasion the King of Scotland was enraged because French pirates were attacking Scottish ships at sea. The King asked Scot to go to the King of France and demand that he order them to stop. Instead of packing his bags and making preparations, he opened his 'Book of Might' and by reading a spell from it he turned one of his assistant spirits into a black horse. He jumped on its back and flew straight to Paris. He delivered his message but just as the King was about to say that no such command would be given, Scot asked him not to make his final decision until he had heard the black horse stamp its foot three times. The French King thought he was mad but complied as he was curious as to what might happen. At the first hoof-stroke all the bells of Paris began ringing. This extraordinary happening failed to change the King's mind. At the second hoof-stroke three towers in the King's palace crashed to the ground. By now the King was less confident and when the black horse raised its hoof to stamp for a third time the King cried, 'Hold! That beast will have the whole place down! Go and tell the King of Scotland that his ships will not be troubled by Frenchmen again.' Scot returned to Scotland on the horse, flying through the air in haste to tell his King of his success.

Sir Michael occasionally enjoyed the pleasures of the chase. When hares were scarce he used an old woman who lived in a cottage on his land and who, in return for his protection, agreed in such emergencies to turn herself into a hare and be chased by the dogs for the amusement of their master. The old lady always managed to elude the dogs. However, one day a strange hound belonging to one of the party was amongst the pack. He was on the leash so Sir Michael had no hesitation in starting as usual. Just as the hare woman was beginning to get away from her pursuers someone cut the leash which held the strange dog. Off went the hound in pursuit and soon overtook the hare, but by this time they were near a small hut on the moor and she was observed entering the hut by leaping through a small window in the gable end. But she hasn't escaped without injury, having been slightly wounded by the dog. It was remarked on by the neighbours that the old woman had a limp ever after, which stopped her enacting the part of the hare for the amusement of the wizard and his guests.

Another day while hunting Sir Michael felt hungry and, spying a house nearby, sent a servant to ask for bread or a bannock. The gudewife replied she had none in the house but the blazing fire, smoking girdle and particular smell of burnt meal, so obvious to the senses of every Scotsman, assured him that she had lied. He returned to his master and reported what had happened. Sir Michael, taking a charm, the Devil's Buckie Shell, from his pocket, gave it to his servant and told him to return to the farmhouse and put it above the lintel of the door without being seen. No sooner had he done this than the charm began to work. The old woman was seized with an unstoppable fit of dancing. She whirled and birled around the chimney, chanting at the same time at the top of her lungs:

'Sir Michael Scot's man
Came seekin' bread and gat nane.'

In the meantime, the farmer began to wonder why his wife had failed to send the shearer's dinner to the fields and so sent a young servant lassie to find out why. The girl had no sooner crossed the threshold than she too began to caper around the chimney with the same vigour as her mistress. Because the lassie didn't come back the farmer decided to go himself and find out what was happening. Before going in though he had a look through the window and saw his wife and the servant dancing like five year olds. Determined to punish them for such unseemly behaviour he strode in but no sooner had he passed under the Buckie than he too was compelled to join the ladies. The dance had now become an uproarious threesome reel made even more so by the chanting of the auld woman.

Later in the day Sir Michael sent his servant back to the house to retrieve the charm from above the door. This done the three dancers dropped from sheer exhaustion, where they fell fast asleep. From then on they vowed never to cross Sir Michael again.

On another occasion Sir Michael was said to have sent a manservant to the Eildon Hills to retrieve his magic book from a fellow wizard he had lent it to. Before he set out on this important mission he was compelled to swear that he would not open the clasps and look inside. But his curiosity was too powerful to be quashed by either faith or fear. By the time he had reached a secluded spot near to home he had succumbed and done what he had long dreamed of, taken a sly peep into the mysterious book. No sooner had he opened it than a swarm of fiends flew out from between the pages, screeching and yelling for employment, crying out to the astonished messenger, 'Work! Work! Work!'

Seeing the Windygates Hill in front of him and remembering the many exhausting ascents he had made on errands for his master, he decided to give them the task of creating a passage through the hill by cutting it in half. He scarcely had time to congratulate himself when back they came as insistent as ever exclaiming 'Work! Work! Work!' Looking east he found their task already completed. What was he to do? It was obvious that if he didn't quickly find another task they would set upon him and no doubt make cat meat of him as it wasn't in their nature to be idle. So he packed them off to the beach at Kirkcaldy to make ropes out of the plentiful supply of sand to be found there. But though they could achieve wonders they couldn't accomplish impossibilities so after an unsuccessful attempt at rope-making, they returned in a very bad humour demanding more rational employment. He now much regretted his actions but as the demons were about to tear him apart Sir Michael arrived on the scene and with a spell sent the demons back into the book – all except one, who was dispatched through the air to Padua with the hapless servant and the instructions to see that he was punished for presuming to practise magic without a diploma.

Many other 'natural' features around Kirkcaldy are attributed to the work of Sir Michael and his demons. The den which runs up from Kirkcaldy and which the railway crosses near Dunniker Mill was produced when he was being pursued by a demon he had offended. To end the pursuit or to get ahead of his enemy he 'caused the earth to yawn at that spot' and it has never since been closed. Local tradition also says the road up to Balwearie Castle was created by his demons.

THE PITTENWEEM WITCHES

In the year 1704 a small, sleepy fishing village in Fife became the scene of perhaps one of the most notorious cases in the history of Scottish witchcraft. The savage brutality meted out to the victims was incredible, even for those dark days.

The tragic tale began when Beatrix Laing asked the sixteen-year-old son of a local blacksmith in Pittenweem to forge her some nails. The boy, Patrick Morton, explained that he was busy on an urgent job but would make the nails as soon as he had finished the work he was engaged upon. Beatrix Laing went away muttering under her breath and the young lad was convinced that she was threatening him with evil.

The following day the boy saw her throwing hot embers into a basin of cold water and was immediately convinced that he was being bewitched. In a few days he had lost his normally healthy appetite and, not surprisingly, eventually became so weak that he fell ill and was confined to bed. As days passed Patrick became subject to fits, his stomach became swollen and he had great difficulty in breathing. In his weakened and feverish condition he became subject to strange and frightening hallucinations, and was firmly convinced that Satan himself kept appearing at the foot of his bed.

The local minister, a certain Revd Patrick Cowper, regularly visited the sick boy and appears to have played upon his already overworked imagination by recounting lurid tales of witchcraft and spell-casting. Eventually, with suitable help from the minister, the young boy accused Beatrix Laing of being a witch and of having cast an evil spell upon him. In addition, he also gave the minister several other names of local villagers and declared that they were also in league with the Powers of Darkness.

Eager to play his part in fighting the forces of the Devil, the minister immediately summoned the members of his presbytery and soon convinced them that Beatrix Laing and her unholy accomplices should all be brought to justice. Although the accused woman was an important person in the village, being the wife of the former village treasurer, she was immediately arrested, as were the other suspects. Before a committee could even be organised to examine them the bailie of Pittenweem placed them in the local gaol and deputised the worst drunkards in the village to guard them. It appears that although it was common knowledge that the deputised guards were not only drunkards but men of extremely low character, the minister himself ordered them to submit the women to every kind of disgusting degradation possible, including the vilest forms of cruel torture. Beatrix Laing was forced to stay awake for five days and nights and eventually confessed to being a witch. She also named Isobel Adam, Janet Cornfoot and a Mistress Lawson, along with several others, as being followers of the Devil.

When the unfortunate woman was released from the torturers she immediately retracted her forced confession, and this infuriated the minister who instantly had her beaten then locked in the village stocks. With the hysterical behaviour of the local minister and other members of the council as an example, it is hardly surprising that the rest of the inhabitants of Pittenweem promptly followed suit and subjected the poor woman to further savage indignities. When she was eventually released from the stocks Beatrix Laing was thrown into the thieves' hole, a dungeon in the local gaol which had neither windows nor any form of lighting. She spent the next five months in solitary confinement.

The remainder of the accused were each brutally tortured until they had confessed to their wicked crimes. The so-called trial dragged wearily on for months and during this time one of the accused, Thomas Brown, starved to death in his dungeon. Some of the more intelligent and enlightened members of the community tried to persuade their fellow commissioners that the accused should be set free and that the only real crime committed had been the stupidity and brutality of the villagers of Pittenweem. Eventually it was agreed that Beatrix Laing and one or two others should be fined the sum of five shillings and set free. Hardly had this happened when a mob chased Beatrix Laing from the village. The minister immediately brought fresh charges against those still in custody. Beatrix Laing managed to reach St Andrews but died in a few months as a result of her ill-treatment while in captivity.

Janet Cornfoot, however, was tortured again and Patrick Cowper himself administered a number of brutal floggings in order to extract a confession. A few days later Janet managed to escape from prison and took refuge with one of the families in the village. When news of her escape became known, the inhabitants of Pittenweem became mad with rage and every house was frantically searched until she was discovered. The terrified woman was dragged to the beach, her hands and feet were tightly bound and a long rope was fastened to her waist. One end of the rope was attached to a ship lying offshore and a crowd of men held the other end. Urged on by the minister she was swung backwards and forwards in the sea until she was almost drowned. Eventually the hysterical mob dragged her onto the sand where blows were rained upon her helpless body by everyone who could get close enough to touch her. A heavy wooden door was placed on top of her and then piles of stones and boulders were heaped upon the door until she was literally pressed to death. Even then the bloodthirsty mob was not satisfied and a horse and sledge were ridden backwards and forwards several times over her body. The local authorities refused to intervene and as a final indignity Patrick Cowper refused to give the dead woman a Christian burial. Incredible though it may be, no action was ever taken to bring any of Janet

Cornfoot's murderers to justice, even after Patrick Morton had confessed that his accusations had been totally false.

THE SPAEWIFE OF CARNBEE

In the spring of 1866 Eliza McGill, resident of Carnbee in the Presbytery of St Andrews, died at the advanced age of ninety-three. Lizzie's father and her whole family were highly respectable and quite well-off. It is said though that in her younger days Lizzie was seen to be of a wayward and impulsive disposition which led her into certain behaviour and habits that lost her the respect and help of her friends, and may have led her to be accused of witchcraft. Out of necessity she appears, eventually, to have been persuaded to modify her conduct and to use her talents to take on the role of fortune-teller, which she is known to have practised with success for more than half a century. For this long period almost everyone, far and near, knew her as a spaewife of no ordinary knowledge. Lizzie was no imposter because she seemed to have sincere faith in her profession. She would often exclaim with solemn fervour, 'The gift I hae is frae aboon an' what He gies, daurna be hidit.'

It was common for young lassies and staid matrons alike to make their way to Lizzie's cottage about twilight to have their fortunes spaed or told.

About ten years before her death, when the prospects of the herring fishing were discouraging in the extreme, a shapely young lassie belonging to Pittenweem went one evening to consult Lizzie. The lassie went with a long face but returned radiant with smiles for the wise woman had said that 'altho' it was to be an awfu' puir draw, yet her ain folk were tae hae a grand haul next evening.' And, true to the auld wife's prediction, the crew which she was interested in returned with a splendid prize from the fishing ground, followed of course with an increase in fame for Lizzie.

On another occasion a fisher wife in St Monans had been given a sovereign by her husband which, being in a hurry, she had put by the bedside. Going later to get it she was puzzled and very upset to find the gold piece gone. She looked everywhere and asked everyone about the lost treasure but with no luck, it couldn't be found. Much distressed the poor woman thought of the spaewife of Carnbee and, adjusting her cap and putting on a clean apron, was soon on her way to see Lizzie. Lizzie's words fell on her troubled spirit like oil on a stormy sea for she was told that in the course of a day or two the sovereign would again be in her hand. And so it was. On pulling her husband's sea boots from under the bed the coin fell from the toe of one of them.

On yet another occasion a cheap trip by the steamer *Xantho* from Anstruther to Leith was advertised. Many of the working folk and their friends arranged to visit Leith and Edinburgh. Unfortunately, the trip was to take place when the farmers of the district were very busy with the sowing of the neeps and of course the workforce was needed. For the purpose of keeping the men at home, Lizzie was persuaded to circulate a rumour round the East Neuk, to the effect that the steamer and all on board were to perish in a fearful gale. The servants were so greatly alarmed by the prediction that they decided to remain at home. The most remarkable feature of the affair is that on the day in question a violent gale arose which prevented the steamer returning to Anstruther until the next morning. The non-arrival of the steamer was a cause of much alarm to the friends of those on board and an old worthy was heard to exclaim with respect to the prediction, 'A dinnae believe in sic things myself, but some wey or ither, they aye come true.' And probably that's what most folk thought.

The Witch of Fife

Once, a long time ago in the Kingdom of Fife, there lived a gudeman and his wife. The old man was a quiet and hard-working soul but his wife was so skeerie and flighty that the neighbours used to nudge each other and whisper that they feared she might be a witch. And her husband was afraid that it might be true because she had a curious habit of disappearing in the evening and staying out all night and when she did come back in the morning she looked quite white and tired, as if she had travelled far or worked hard. Try as he might to watch her carefully and find out where she went and what she did he never managed to do so because she always slipped out of the door while he wasn't looking, and before he had reached it to follow her she had vanished completely.

Eventually, one day, the husband decided it was time he knew, so he asked her right out if she was a witch. But his blood ran cold when, without hesitation, she answered that she was and if he promised not to let anyone know, the next time she went out on one of her adventures she would tell him all about it. Well the old man agreed because he thought it was only right that a husband should know all about what his wife got up to.

He didn't have long to wait because the very next week it was a new moon and the time when witches like to venture out. That very night his wife vanished and didn't return until daybreak.

When he asked her where she had been, it was with great excitement and pleasure that she told her story. She had met four other companions in the old kirkyard where they had mounted branches of the green bay tree and stalks of hemlock, which had immediately turned into horses carrying them, swift as the wind, over the country, hunting the foxes, the weasels and the owls. Then they had swum the loch and come to the top of the Lomond Hills, where they had dismounted and

drunk beer made in no earthly brewery from little horn cups made by no mortal hand. Then a wee man had appeared from under a great mossy stone with a tiny set of bagpipes under his arm and played such wonderful music that, at the sound of it, the very fish jumped out of the loch below, and the stoats crept out of their holes, and the crows and herons came and sat on the trees in the darkness just to listen. The witches danced until they were so tired that they could hardly hang on to their horses on the way home.

The gudeman listened to this long story in silence, shaking his head from time to time, and when it was finished all that he said was, 'And what good has all that dancing done you? Would you not have been better at home in bed with your dear little bairns and me?'

The next new moon saw the wife disappearing again. When she returned this time she told of how she and her friends had taken cockleshells from the beach and turned them into boats and had sailed over the stormy sea to Norway. There they had mounted invisible horses of wind and had ridden over mountains, glens and glaciers until they reached the snow-covered lands of the Lapps lying under a cloak of snow. Here all the elves, fairies and mermaids of the North were holding a festival with warlocks, broonies, pixies and even the Phantom Hunters themselves, who are never seen by mortal eyes. The Witches of Fife joined in with the dancing, feasting and singing. She told how the warlock men and weird women had washed them with witch-water, distilled from the moorland dew till their beauty bloomed like the Lapland rose that grows wild in the forest. Then, soft in the arms of the warlock men, they had lain down to sleep. But more importantly, they were taught certain magical words which, when spoken, would carry them through the air and undo all bolts and bars and gain them entry to any place they wanted to be. They had returned home, delighted with the knowledge they had been given.

'You're lying,' cried out the old man, 'you're lying. The ugliest wife on the shores of Fife is bonnier than you! Why would the warlock men lie with you? And what took you to such a cauld land? Would you no' have been warmer at home in bed wi' me?'

But the next time he took a wee bit more notice of what she said, because she told of how they had met in the cottage of one of her friends and how, having heard that the Lord Bishop of Carlisle had a very fine wine cellar, they had each placed a foot on the pan hook over the fire and had spoken the magic words they had learned from the Elves of Lapland. As soon as the words were out of their mouths they disappeared up the chimney like whiffs of smoke and sailed through the air like little clouds to land at the bishop's palace in Carlisle.

There the doors flew open and they went down into the bishop's wine cellar, where they sampled the fine wines, returning to Fife, fine sober old women, by daybreak.

When he heard this the old man took notice. He liked a fine wine himself but it seldom came his way. 'You are a wife to be proud of,' he cried. 'Maybe you could tell me these words? I would like to go and sample the bishop's wine myself.'

'Na, na,' she replied. 'I couldn't do that because you might tell it over again and the whole world would be turned upside down with folk going into each other's houses whenever they pleased.' And although he tried to persuade her with all the soft words he could think of, she wouldn't give up her secret.

But he had a sly side and the thought of the bishop's wine stayed with him, so night after night he visited the other cottages in the hope that he would catch his wife and her friends meeting there. It took a long time but at last his trouble was rewarded. One night they assembled and in low tones, amid chuckles of laughter as they reminded each other of their adventures in Lapland, one by one they climbed onto the sooty hook, repeated the magic words, and disappeared up the lum. 'I can do that too,' he thought, crawling out of his hiding place and running to the fire, where he put his foot on the hook and repeated the magic words he had heard. He too flew up the lum and out into the night air after his wife and her companions. And, as witches never look over their shoulders, he wasn't noticed until they reached the bishop's cellar. They weren't pleased when they discovered he was amongst them but what could they do? They got on with enjoying themselves, sampling the wines as before. But while they just took a little here and a little there, the husband was not so cautious. He drank so much that he was fast asleep on the floor when the time came to leave. Thinking to teach him a lesson, they left him there to be discovered the next morning by the bishop's servants. Much surprised to find him in a locked cellar, he was dragged before the bishop himself, who asked for an explanation. The poor old man was so confused that all he could say was that he came from Fife 'on the midnight wind'. Hearing that, the bishop declared he must be a warlock and ordered him to be burnt alive.

Well the poor man now wished he had minded his own business and stayed at home. But it was too late. He was dragged outside and chained to a great iron stake. Piles of wood were placed around his feet and set alight. As the flames crept up he thought his last hour had come. Just then there was a swish and a flutter of wings and a bird appeared in the sky, swooping down to perch for a moment on the old man's shoulder to whisper in his ear. The old man's heart jumped for joy as he realised this was his wife with her magic words. He called them out and immediately the chains fell away and the old man sailed off into the air, much to the amazement of the crowd. And when he found himself safely at home once more he vowed to leave his wife to her own devices from then on and never try to find out her secrets.

GLOSSARY

aboon: above

aince: once

aucht: eight

baffies: slippers

bannock: oatmeal scone

baw-bee: coin

bladderskate: boaster

blether: a talkative person

boon: reward

braw: good

breid: bread

buckie: type of shell

cannae: can't

cheuching: exclamation made while dancing

clag: cover with mud or clay

claithes: clothes

cled: dressed in

clype: telltale or gossip

contrar: oppose

cowp: turn upside down

dad: strike

daurna: daren't

De'il: Devil

dings: beats with a stick

dominie: school master

dwam: daydream

dyke: wall

fower knockit: four cornered, square

gang: go

gly'd: cross-eyed

gude: good, respectable

gudeman: head of a household, farmer

gudewife: mistress of a house, farmer's wife

hallanshaker: tramp or beggar

heuching: exclamation made while dancing

howk: dig up

ilka: every

ill-pretts: nasty tricks

kailyard: kitchen garden

ken: know

kirk: church

limmer bead: piece of amber

lug: ear

lulls: bagpipes

lum: chimney

malison: curse

maukins: hare

maun: must

muck-a-byre: a derogatory term for a farmer, someone who cleans out the cowshed

neeps: turnips

partans: crabs

puckle: a few

sair: sore

shew: sew

sic: such

skeerie: nervous, agitated

smiddy: blacksmith

sowans: a dish of oat husks and fine meal

spaewife: fortune teller

spier: ask in a nosey way

taen: taken

tatties: potatoes

tocher: dowry

weel: well

wheesht: ask to keep quiet

whulk: whelk, shellfish

wire in: eat up, tuck in

wraught: worked

yett: gate

BIBLIOGRAPHY

Bruce, George, *Wrecks and Reminiscences of St Andrews Bay*, St
  Andrews, 1826
Buchan, Peter, *Ancient Ballads and Songs of Northern Scotland*,
  Edinburgh: W. Aitken, 1828
Chalmers, Revd Peter, *Historical and Statistical Account of
  Dunfermline*, Edinburgh: Blackwood & Son, 1844
Chambers, Robert, *The Popular Rhymes of Scotland*,
  Edinburgh: W. & R. Chambers, 1826
Gulland, C., *The Lomond Hills – A Poem*, Cupar, 1877
Henderson, Ebenezer, *The Annals of Dunfermline and Vicinity*,
  Glasgow: John Tweed, 1879
Jack, John, *An Historical Account of St Monans, Fifeshire*,
  Cupar: J.S. Tullis, 1844
Mackay, A.J.G., *A History of Fife and Kinross*, Edinburgh:
  Blackwood & Son, 1896
Small, Revd Andrew, *Interesting Roman Antiquities Recently
  Discovered in Fife*, Edinburgh: J. Anderson & Co., 1823
Wilkie, James, *Bygone Fife*, Edinburgh: William Blackwood &
  Son, 1931

Scottish Storytelling Forum

The Scottish Storytelling Centre is delighted to be associated with the *Folk Tales* series developed by The History Press. Its talented storytellers continue the Scottish tradition, revealing the regional riches of Scotland in these volumes. These include the different environments, languages and cultures encompassed in our big wee country. The Scottish Storytelling Centre provides a base and communications point for the national storytelling network, along with national networks for Traditional Music and Song and Traditions of Dance, all under the umbrella of TRACS (Traditional Arts and Culture Scotland). See www.scottishstorytellingcentre.co.uk for further information. The Traditional Arts community of Scotland is also delighted to be working with all the nations and regions of Great Britain and Ireland through the *Folk Tales* series.